D1581918

# We Are What We Think

*Also by James Geary*

The Body Electric:
An Anatomy of the New Bionic Senses

# We Are What We Think

A Journey Through the Wisest and Wittiest Sayings in the World

*James Geary*

JOHN MURRAY

© James Geary 2005

First published in Great Britain in 2005 by John Murray (Publishers)
A division of Hodder Headline

The right of James Geary to be identified as the Author of the Work has been
asserted by him in accordance with the Copyright, Designs and Patents Act 1988.

1

A CIP catalogue record for this title is available from the British Library

ISBN 0 7195 6134 5

Typeset in 10.5/13.5 Monotype Sabon by Servis Filmsetting Ltd, Manchester

Printed and bound by Clays Ltd, St. Ives, plc

Hodder Headline policy is to use papers that are natural, renewable and recyclable
products and made from wood grown in sustainable forests. The logging and
manufacturing processes are expected to conform to the environmental regulations
of the country of origin.

John Murray (Publishers)
338 Euston Road
London NW1 3BH

'Life consists of what a man is thinking of all day.'

*– Ralph Waldo Emerson*

# Contents

*Introduction* Guessing is more fun than knowing

*The Confessions of an Aphorism Addict*

If not for an aphorism by W. H. Auden, I might never have met my wife.

I was in my final year at university, studying a haphazard mix of poetry, philosophy and literature. Since the college I attended placed special emphasis on the performing arts, I periodically staged little happenings based on things I was writing or thinking about at the time. One of these performances involved lugging about a dozen extremely large and heavy stones into the dining hall during dinner one evening and heaping them into a small cairn. I stood on top of the cairn, tapped a fork lightly on the rim of a glass until I had the room's attention, and spat a handful of smaller stones from my mouth. Then I lugged the big stones back outside again. It sounds absurd now, but at the time I thought I was making a pretty profound statement – in that enigmatic and grandiose way only undergraduates can – about the stubbornness of language, the impossibility of ever really saying what we mean.

It was at a similar event that I first encountered the woman who would become my wife.

For this performance, though, the only thing I carried into the cafeteria was the world itself – in the shape of a desktop globe from which I had neatly excised the Arctic Circle, so that the top of the earth came off like the lid of a biscuit tin. I had dropped dozens of little slips of paper into the globe, each one bearing a short, smart, snappy saying – either one I had composed myself, or one from a famous writer. As I strolled through the dining hall, I approached people as they ate and asked them to reach in and pick a phrase from the globe. The only catch: everyone had to read the aphorism aloud. I wouldn't leave the table until they did.

I was an aspiring aphorist at the time, so the globe contained what I considered some of my best lines:

Never trust an animal – no matter how many legs it has.

Young people should picnic in active volcanoes.

There are certain mistakes we enjoy so much we are always willing to repeat them.

There is not much room for error in an eggshell.

Not many people live in the desert.

And, my personal favourite:

Sometimes, two goldfish in a bowl are enough.

But the globe also contained lots of great aphorisms from some of my favourite authors, including this one from W. H. Auden:

Knowledge may have its purposes, but guessing is always more fun than knowing.

My wife-to-be – whom I had never actually met at this point – picked this saying from the globe and, after some initial hesitation and embarrassment, read it aloud. Then I moved on to the next table and distributed about two dozen more aphorisms before the performance ended.

The next day, I found a little slip of paper in my mailbox. It read:

In some cases, knowing is much more fun than guessing.

That was it. The scrap of paper, torn from a larger sheet, displayed no name and no other message. But I remembered who had selected the W. H. Auden saying, and later that day spotted my wife-to-be in the hallway on her way to class. I was waiting on the landing for my class to begin and she was walking down the stairs. As she passed, I leaned over the railing and said: 'You're right. In some cases, knowing *is* much more fun than guessing.' She blushed a bit, and kept on walking. But that evening, she appeared unannounced in the doorway to my room – and the rest is history.

Aphorisms have changed my life, and not just because I have one to thank for meeting my wife. I've been inspired and enthralled by aphorisms since I was about eight, when I first encountered the form in the 'Quotable Quotes' section of *Reader's Digest*.

My parents were faithful subscribers to *Reader's Digest*, and I would often find back copies of the magazine lying crumpled and slightly damp on the bathroom floor. Quotable Quotes are brief inspirational sayings – usually by celebrities, television personalities or statesmen, but often by authors and sometimes by ordinary people – that dispense advice about things like overcoming adversity, dealing with disappointment or grief, and coping with family life. This one, by American 'TV counsellor' Dr Phil McGraw, culled at random from a recent issue of the magazine, exemplifies the style:

If you marry for money, you will earn every penny.

I was just starting to become a serious reader, so these titbits were exactly the right length for my pre-adolescent attention span. At the time, of course, I didn't know an aphorism from an aphrodisiac, but there was something about these brief, unusual sayings that attracted me. I loved the puns, paradoxes and clever turns of phrase. And I was amazed at how such a compact statement could contain so much significance. Reading a really good Quotable Quote was like looking into a kaleidoscope; after twisting it around in my mind for a while, I was surprised at how many different meanings I could find.

The best quotes were powerful, majestic, inspirational and faintly oracular. And they were funny too, even though the topics they dealt with often involved some kind of personal

4

tragedy. These really were words to live by, and when I was about thirteen I started collecting them.

In the beginning, it wasn't immediately clear to me *how* to collect aphorisms. You either have to have a very good memory or make some note of the sayings as you read them. I opted for the latter method. I took down the poster of George Harrison on my wall – the one from *All Things Must Pass* with him wearing a big floppy hat and looking very hirsute – flipped it around, hung it back up and started writing the aphorisms on the back. As a collector, I was very much like the person described by the eighteenth-century French aphorist Nicolas Chamfort:

Most collectors of verses and sayings proceed as though they were eating cherries or oysters, choosing the best first, and ending by eating them all.

My appetite for aphorisms was enormous, so when the George Harrison poster filled up I moved on to David Bowie and Pink Floyd. The collection grew until I was in my early twenties, when I developed a taste for collecting books instead. But the posters still hang on the wall of my study. The paper is browned and cracking now; the corners torn away by attaching and then removing so much Sellotape. Quotations crowd into every available space. The earliest entries, written in red ink in my neat but jagged teenage script, are so faded with age that they're barely legible.

Reading these posters today is like travelling back in time, like leafing through a scrapbook of intellectual snapshots.

Each quote triggers a host of memories and associations about where I was when I first read it, what I thought and believed at the time, who I was trying to become.

The George Harrison poster, for example, has lots of extracts from books by Ayn Rand, J. D. Salinger, Kurt Vonnegut and Henry David Thoreau. This was my alien-hermit phase when, like Thoreau, I would spend long summer days communing with nature and my own socially inept self at my version of Walden Pond in the suburbs of Philadelphia. Pink Floyd sports mostly William Blake, John Keats, Aldous Huxley, Sylvia Plath and Rainer Maria Rilke, plus a nice little quip from Don Staley, my secondary school English teacher. This was my romantic-solipsist stage, when my sole aim was to plumb the depths of my emotions and storm the stubborn doors of perception. And Bowie has such heavyweights as Heidegger, Wittgenstein, Kierkegaard, Nietzsche and the occasional Zen koan – my existentialist-nihilist period, when I rashly imagined I'd seen through the world and to prove the point put on philosophical stunts like spitting a handful of stones from my mouth.

Some of these aphorisms seem a little shallow now. Ayn Rand's exhortations about the virtues of selfishness, for example, no longer move me. But others are still as compelling as when I first copied them down. I still refer to them in times of trouble, doubt or crisis. They pop into my head when I least expect it. And they still retain their power to inspire and amuse:

Mirrors would do well to reflect a little more before sending back images. – *Jean Cocteau*

6

Life is like playing a violin solo in public and learning the instrument as one goes on. – *Samuel Butler*

I have often been forced to my knees by the overwhelming conviction that there was no place else to go. – *Abraham Lincoln*

I never let school interfere with my education. – *Mark Twain*

The effect of studying masterpieces is to make me admire and do otherwise. – *Gerard Manley Hopkins*

And this phrase, which has become a constant refrain in my head, recurring every morning as I walk to work:

The difference between a rut and a grave is the depth.

This aphorism from a somewhat improbable source – Gerald Burrill, once the Episcopal Bishop of Chicago – has been a fixture of my thinking ever since I scrawled it on the back of that George Harrison poster almost thirty years ago. It's a chilling phrase – a graphic warning that hebetude is the enemy of joy, that drudgery is habit-forming – and it's suddenly there in my mind as I make my daily pilgrimage to the Underground station.

As a teenager, this saying appealed to me because it summed up my aversion to constricting social conventions, to the way my peers and I were funnelled through church and school into narrow lifestyles ánd deadening careers. Today it still keeps me looking for less-trodden paths. As I trudge to the Tube every

7

morning, this aphorism reminds me that my job, however fun, frustrating, exhausting or exhilarating, is not my life, that less travelled roads offer the most stunning views, that open minds invite surprise.

To make sure I really walk the talk, though, I regularly vary my route to work. I skip my usual Tube stop and get off somewhere else; I take a different path to the office; or I simply walk on the other side of the street – small alterations that keep me off the well-worn path and change my point of view. Fresh perspectives can squeeze through even the slightest breaks in routine.

This little morning ritual is one reason I love aphorisms, and why I believe they can change your life. Aphorisms are not the warm and fuzzy phrases found in greeting cards. They are much more brusque, confrontational and subversive. You don't curl up with a good book of aphorisms; they leap off the page and unfurl inside you.

Aphorisms aren't meant to make you feel good about yourself, either. More often than not they are cynical and acerbic, an antidote to the bland, relentlessly upbeat nostrums in self-help guides and inspirational literature. They definitely do not cheer you up. Instead, aphorisms fulfil a much more difficult and important task: they make you question everything you think and do. Aphorisms deliver the short sharp shock of an old forgotten truth. They keep your mind in shape by making you wonder every morning whether you're simply walking to work or digging your own grave.

Aphorisms are spurs to action. It's not enough to just read one and murmur sagely to yourself, 'How true, how true.' Aphorisms make you want to do something; admiring them without putting them into practice is like learning to read music but neglecting to play an instrument.

This is how aphorisms can change your life. But how do you recognize an aphorism when you read it? And what makes an aphorism different from other types of sayings, such as adages, apophthegms, axioms, bromides, dictums, epigrams, mottoes, parables, platitudes, precepts, proverbs, quips, quotations, soundbites, slogans, truisms and witticisms?

Ironically for the world's shortest form of literature, a compact definition of the aphorism is impossible. There are, however, five laws an aphorism must obey to make the grade. By these signs shall ye know them.

## The Five Laws of Aphorisms

The philosopher J. S. Mill once observed that there are two kinds of wisdom in the world: 'In the one, every age in which science flourishes surpasses, or ought to surpass, its predecessors; of the other, there is nearly an equal amount in all ages.' The first kind of wisdom is scientific. It consists in what we know about the world and how it works, and how we put that knowledge to use through technology. Since the Industrial Revolution at least, each age has surpassed the scientific achievements of its predecessors with astonishing speed.

Mills calls the second type 'the wisdom of ages', a somewhat exalted term for what we've collectively learned about human nature through the experience of individuals across thousands of years of history. This kind of knowledge is unsystematic, consists in psychological rather than empirical facts, and is present in more or less equal amounts in every historical period. So Dr Phil McGraw potentially has just about as much – or as little – of this kind of wisdom at his disposal as the Taoist sage Lao Tzu, who lived in China about six hundred years before Christ. 'The form in which this kind of wisdom most naturally embodies itself', Mill concludes, 'is that of aphorisms.'

Why aphorisms? Because they're just the right size to hold the swift insights and fresh observations that are the raw data of the wisdom of the ages. Aphorisms are literature's hand luggage. Light and compact, they fit easily into the overhead compartment of your brain and contain everything you need to get through a rough day at the office or a dark night of the soul. They are, as the nineteenth-century author John Morley observed, 'the guiding oracles which man has found out for himself in that great business of ours, of learning how to be, to do, to do without, and to depart'.

Here, then, are the five laws by which an aphorism performs its oracular work.

## 1. It Must Be Brief

If brevity is the soul of wit, as Shakespeare observed in one of his many aphoristic insights, then concision is the aphorism's heart. Aphorisms must work quickly because they are meant for use in emergencies. We're most in need of aphorisms at times of distress or joy, ecstasy or anguish. And in cases of spiritual or emotional urgency, brevity is the best policy.

The author of *The Cloud of Unknowing*, a spiritual instruction manual written by an anonymous English monk in the latter half of the fourteenth century, knew this when he advised his students:

Short prayer penetrates heaven.

*The Cloud of Unknowing* was composed as an aid to contemplation, and it's packed with sound spiritual guidance and sweet admonitions for young men just entering the monastic life. The book is made up of 75 very short chapters, with amusing and sometimes impenetrable titles such as 'The three things the contemplative beginner must practise: reading, thinking, and praying' and 'A man's outlook is wonderfully altered through the spiritual experience of this nothing in its nowhere'. Each chapter is written in very simple, direct prose, in an avuncular tone that highlights the author's wisdom, equanimity and good humour.

The book's title refers to our imperfect knowledge of God, but the author urges his readers to 'hammer away at this high cloud of unknowing' through meditation and prayer. *The Cloud*'s language mostly clings very close to the ground, however, and the book is replete with down-to-earth tips on how monks should pray silently to themselves throughout the day and how they can find the sacred in the most mundane daily chores.

Chapter 37 explains by means of a surprisingly commonplace metaphor why pithiness is next to godliness:

A man or a woman, suddenly frightened by fire, or death, or what you will, is suddenly in his extremity of spirit driven hastily and by

11

necessity to cry or pray for help. And how does he do it? Not, surely, with a spate of words; not even in a single word of two syllables! Why? He thinks it wastes too much time to declare his urgent need and his agitation. So he bursts out in his terror with one little word, and that of a single syllable: 'Fire!' it may be, or 'Help!' Just as this little word stirs and pierces the ears of the hearers more quickly, so too does a little word of one syllable, when it is not merely spoken or thought, but expresses also the intention in the depth of our spirit.

Aphorists are people who've experienced 'extremity of spirit', and aphorisms are read by people in the same predicament. They are terse and to the point because their message is urgent. There's no time to waste.

An aphorism can be anything from a few words to a few sentences long; the French call the former an *aperçu*, a swift, sweeping insight, and the latter a *pensée*, a longer, more leisurely train of thought. But only a fool makes a speech in a burning house. That's why the author of *The Cloud of Unknowing* hammered his meaning home in such short, vivid phrases. When you find yourself *in extremis*, aphorisms tell you everything you need to know. The rest is just salad dressing.

## 2. *It Must Be Definitive*

In *The Life of Samuel Johnson*, James Boswell describes the great English lexicographer as 'a man of most dreadful appearance . . . He is very slovenly in his dress and speaks with a most uncouth voice . . . He has a great humour and is a worthy man. But his dogmatic roughness of manners is disagreeable'. What Boswell fails to mention, however, is that a little dogmatism is no bad thing when you're compiling a dictionary, as Johnson was from 1746 to 1755.

Johnson was famously convinced of his own opinions, and not shy about declaiming them, essential qualities for both the lexicographer and the aphorist. After all, a definition – like an aphorism – must be, well, definitive. In fact, the term itself is derived from the Greek words *apo* (meaning 'from') and *horos* (meaning 'boundary' or 'horizon'), so an aphorism is something that marks off or sets apart – that is, a definition.

Aphorisms and definitions assert rather than argue, proclaim rather than persuade, state rather than suggest. Johnson's most famous aphorism:

Patriotism is the last refuge of a scoundrel

wouldn't be nearly as piquant if he had couched it in all kinds of caveats and qualifications.

Of course, aphorisms aren't necessarily a hundred per cent true – Ambrose Bierce, Johnson's twentieth-century counterpart, contends, for example, that patriotism is the scoundrel's *first* refuge – yet they demand assent through the declarative style in which they are expressed. The English essayist William Hazlitt put it well when he wrote of aphorisms, 'There is a peculiar stimulus . . . in this mode of writing. A thought must tell at once, or not at all.'

Because aphorisms must tell at once they often take the form of definitions – x *is* y. There is no deliberation or debate, and no supporting evidence. We must literally take the aphorist at

13

his word. That's usually easy enough because those words are so lucid that they carry their own conviction. Of no one is this more true than Johnson himself, whose aphorisms could easily have served as entries in his dictionary of the English language. Here are two of his less optimistic pronouncements:

Life is a pill which none of us can bear to swallow without gilding.

To build is to be robbed.

Johnson defined the lexicographer as 'a writer of dictionaries, a harmless drudge'. But aphorists are far from harmless. They are troublemakers and iconoclasts, dogmatists whose majestic authority commands consent. They are, by definition, revolutionaries who hold their truths to be self-evident.

## 3. *It Must Be Personal*

In 1955, Alfred Kessler, a physician and collector of the works of G. K. Chesterton, was poking around a used bookstore in San Francisco when he came across a copy of Holbrook Jackson's *Platitudes in the Making*. Jackson, a literary critic and contemporary of Chesterton, had this little book of maxims privately published in 1911. But as Kessler flipped through the pages of the slim volume he realized that this was no ordinary copy of *Platitudes*. Scrawled in bright green pencil beneath each of Jackson's maxims was a handwritten response: either an endorsement of the idea behind the saying or, more often, an emphatic rejection accompanied by an alternative aphorism. For example, penned underneath Jackson's

He who reasons is lost

was the arch retort:

He who never reasons is not worth finding.

Kessler recognized the handwriting, and turning back to the front of the book was startled to read the following inscription: 'To G. K. Chesterton, with esteem from Holbrook Jackson'. Kessler had in his hands Chesterton's personal copy of *Platitudes in the Making*, and the impassioned scratchings in green pencil were Chesteron's ripostes to Jackson's aphorisms. Kessler had stumbled on the greatest discovery of his collecting career, and recovered for Chesterton fans some of the great English author's most incisive sayings.

If you had never read a word by either Jackson or Chesterton – the former now largely forgotten and the latter best remembered for his detective series *The Father Brown Stories* – and *Platitudes* were recited aloud, it would be easy to guess which aphorism was by whom. Jackson fancied himself a modern romantic, an atheist philosopher in the shadow of Nietzsche, so his sayings are filled with disdain for convention and praise for man's impulsive, irrational nature. Pretty typical of Jackson's output is:

Don't think – do.

Chesterton, on the other hand, was a devout Catholic rationalist, as well as a committed socialist and environmentalist long before the latter was a fashionable occupation. He did believe in God and in man's triumph over the baser instincts through reason and morality. So his reply is a fairly accurate summary of his philosophy, too:

Do think! Do!

It's this personal quality which gives aphorisms their power to charm and enrage. An aphorism takes you inside the head of the person who wrote it or said it. 'The thought . . . must be stamped with the hallmark of the mind that thinks it,' as critic and aphorism junkie Logan Pearsall Smith wrote in the introduction to his 1947 anthology of English maxims.

Aphorisms are not bland generalizations about life, the universe and everything but deeply personal and idiosyncratic statements, as unique to an individual as a strand of his or her DNA. This is what distinguishes the form from proverbs, for instance, which are really worn-out aphorisms that have had the identity of the original author rubbed away through repeated use.

The personal touch is important because aphorisms are not bits of uplifting text meant for passive consumption. They are challenging statements that demand a response: either the recognition of a shared insight – what Alexander Pope described as something that 'oft was thought but ne'er so well expressed' – or a rejection and retort. As the Jackson–Chesterton exchange shows, aphorisms are intimate encounters between two minds. If they don't give you a little shock, something isn't right.

Francis Bacon, the English author, politician and scientist, loved aphorisms precisely because of this ability to upset preconceptions. He inherited his affection for the form from his father, who had quotations from the classics carved into the columns of the family manor at Gorhambury, near St Albans just north of London. The younger Bacon recommended the use of aphorisms because they pique curiosity rather than satisfy it, provoke further thought rather than thwart it: 'Aphorisms, representing a knowledge broken, do invite men to enquire farther.'

Aphorisms are like particle accelerators for the mind. When high-energy particles such as electrons and positrons collide inside an accelerator, new particles are created as the energy of the crash is converted into matter. The freshly minted matter spins out from the collision at incredibly high velocities and disintegrates again within about one millionth of a billionth of a billionth of a second. Trying to track the particles in this miniature big bang is like blowing up a haystack and trying to spot a needle as the debris flies past. Inside an aphorism, it is minds which collide and the new matter that spins out at the speed of thought is that elusive thing we call wisdom. Keep your eyes peeled or you'll miss it.

## 4. *It Must Have a Twist*

Outside France, François-René de Chateaubriand – author, adventurer, lover, statesman – is probably best remembered for the meal that eighteenth-century gourmand Jean-Anthelme Brillat-Savarin named after him. Chateaubriand steak, served with mushrooms and Béarnaise sauce, is still standard fare in many a Parisian bistro.

But in his own day Chateaubriand was France's answer to Lord Byron. Like that of his flamboyant British soulmate, Chateaubriand's life was just as famous as his art. Born in Brittany in 1768, he fled the chaos that followed the Revolution and went to America, where he travelled around the Midwest and went back to nature – eighteenth-century-style. Influenced by Jean-Jacques Rousseau's ideal of the 'noble savage', Chateaubriand specialized in exotic descriptions of the natural world and fictional encounters with native Americans. His best-known novels, *Atala* and *René*, melancholic tales of tragic love affairs, are credited with introducing Romanticism to France. Chateaubriand had a long governmental career as well, serving variously as secretary to the embassy at Rome, ambassador to London and eventually Minister of Foreign Affairs.

As an aphorist, Chateaubriand had a wicked way with a turn of phrase. Aphorisms achieve their maximum impact through paradox and sudden reversals of import. Reading a good aphorism is like watching a magic trick: first comes surprise, then comes delight, then you start wondering how the hell the magician did it. Chateaubriand did it through his mastery of the verbal pirouette, as in this remark on what makes an author great:

An original writer is not one who imitates nobody, but one whom nobody can imitate.

All Chateaubriand's aphorisms have this kind of syllogistic construction. He sets up a seemingly simple equation and once you think you've deduced the answer he slips in exactly the opposite conclusion. Instead of a passionate endorsement of romantic love, we get a cold assessment of our instinct for self-deception:

As long as the heart preserves desire, the mind preserves illusion.

Sometimes, you've got to step lively to keep up with Chateaubriand's turnings. The following aphorism really annoyed me on first reading, mostly because I initially took it to mean something pretty trivial, such as infatuation fades with familiarity:

Love decreases when it ceases to increase.

Why bother writing an aphorism about that, I thought. It's too obvious. But then I read it again, and again, and eventually I got it. What Chateaubriand is really saying is that if you're not constantly falling in love with your beloved, then you're already starting to fall out the other side of love.

Like a good joke, a good aphorism has a punchline, a quick verbal or psychological flip, a sudden sting in the tail that gives you a jolt. Both jokes and aphorisms lift you into a wonderful weightless state – that giddy point just after the joke is finished and just before you get it – then abruptly drop you back down to earth in some completely unexpected place. Aphorisms, like jokes, teach the mind to do the twist.

19

## 5. *It Must Be Philosophical*

Friedrich von Schlegel practised the spontaneous-combustion method of philosophical composition. In contrast to earlier thinkers such as Descartes and Spinoza, who devised elaborate and meticulously argued systems, Schlegel liked to publish his thoughts raw, in the form in which they first occurred to him: as aphorisms.

Schlegel jotted down his musings in a notebook and printed them in *Athenaeum*, the literary journal he founded in 1798 with his brother, August Wilhelm. Like Bacon, he believed this kind of fragmented philosophizing more accurately reflected the shifting, scattershot nature of thinking – and the experience of life itself. Aphorisms, he said, are the 'true form of the Universal Philosophy' and contain 'the greatest quantity of thought in the smallest space'.

Born in Hanover in 1771, Schlegel was an early prophet of the Romantic movement in literature. As a teenager, he was apprenticed to a banker in Leipzig but couldn't confine his mind to the rigid credit and debit columns of finance. So he took up the study of literature, comparative philology and Greek antiquity. For him, philosophy consisted of a series of imaginative leaps rather than a sequence of plodding, logical steps; thinking for himself was a continuous pursuit, not an activity that stopped when he arrived at the 'truth':

One can only become a philosopher, not be one. As soon as one thinks one is a philosopher, one stops becoming one.

Aphorisms are signposts along the route to becoming a philosopher. It's a journey we all have to make. Some go gladly; some go recklessly; some go on automatic pilot. Nobody gets a map. It's the oldest trip in the book – from birth to death, from self to world, from known to unknown – but each of us travels it anew, and totally alone. Aphorisms reassure us that someone has been this way before. They entreat us to keep on the path, to avoid the ruts.

Aphorisms are not, however, metaphysical short cuts. As Schlegel says, it's the journey which matters; the destination may not even exist. They are not revision notes on the drama of human life, either, but pieces of a grand mosaic, fragments of the bigger picture we're always striving to glimpse. Schlegel described them like this:

A fragment, like a miniature work of art, has to be entirely isolated from the surrounding world and be complete in itself like a porcupine.

Aphorisms are literary loners, set apart from the world because they're worlds unto themselves. They're like porcupines, bristling with prickly philosophical spines. Rub them the wrong way and you're in for a surprise.

A perfect example of the five laws of the aphorism at work can be seen in the Old Manse in Concord, Massachusetts. In the middle of the nineteenth century, the Old Manse was home to two of America's most distinguished writers. Ralph Waldo Emerson owned the house first and composed his influential essay 'Nature' in the study upstairs. Then came Nathaniel

21

Hawthorne and his wife Sophia. Hawthorne wrote some of his short stories up in Emerson's old study and Sophia, a painter, used to etch little sayings on to the windows of the house with her diamond ring. Two of these inscriptions remain.

In the ground-floor dining room, Sophia noted the fact that her painting *Endymion* was completed here in January 1844. A year later, just below that inscription, she recorded this intimate moment with her baby daughter: 'Una Hawthorne stood on this window sill January 22d 1845 while the trees were all glass chandeliers – a goodly show which she liked much tho' only ten months old.'

On an upstairs window, in Hawthorne's study, Sophia wrote this:

Man's accidents are God's purposes, 1843.

No one knows what prompted Sophia Hawthorne to engrave this phrase on the window. Some scholars suggest it may refer to a miscarriage she had that year after slipping on a patch of ice. There is a sense of grief and resignation about her words, but also of strength and resolution. No easy answer is asked for or given, just a blunt acceptance of events and a determination to either endure or overcome them.

Our need for words of wisdom like this is ancient, as old as 'the wisdom of the ages' itself, which is why the aphorism is the oldest written art form on the planet. The Chinese were at it more than five thousand years ago; the ancient Greek philosophers, Old Testament authors, Buddha, Jesus and Muhammad were all early practitioners, too. This history, told through the lives and aphorisms of some of the form's greatest practitioners (this is a *brief* history, though, so many wonderful aphorists have been regrettably excluded), shows that the aphorism is still as sprightly and as apposite as ever. Even in our modern age of drive-through culture, soporific soundbites and manufactured sentiment, aphorisms retain their power to instigate and inspire, enlighten and enrage, entertain and edify.

Sophia Hawthorne knew this as she stood at her window, looking out at the trees all sheathed in ice, looking through the thin, pale letters she etched on the glass. Aphorisms are fine, incisive sayings that in dark times and in light help us see the world more smartly.

# 1 We are what we think:

## Ancient Sages, Preachers and Prophets

After graduating from college in 1985, I moved to San Francisco, where by day I worked variously as a van driver and typesetter and by night wrote poetry and studied Buddhism and Chinese philosophy. It was in San Francisco that I acquired a taste for Chinese food, and it was in the KK Café – the Chinese joint around the corner from my apartment – that I first had the idea of making fortunes.

Chinese restaurants abound in San Francisco. The food is good, the portions large, the prices cheap – important considerations for an impoverished recent graduate – and at the end of every meal you get a fortune cookie.

I never really liked the taste of these savouries, a cross between desiccated cookie dough and a stale communion wafer. And the fortunes themselves are invariably trite and boring – 'You will make a big trip' or 'Success will soon be yours'. But serving up a little food for thought is the perfect way to end a meal. How much better, though, if the fortunes were actually provocative and interesting. The only solution, I decided, was to write them myself.

After making a few enquiries, I found Golden Gate Fortune Cookies in Ross Alley, a dank, narrow lane off Washington Street in Chinatown. The firm's fortune cookie factory was tiny – the entire workspace was about the size of a large kitchen – but this little establishment churned out a prodigious number of cookies. Cardboard boxes filled with them were stacked to the ceiling along all four walls, a tribute to the productivity of the two small women who silently operated the machinery in opposite corners of the shop. I soon became a regular customer.

To make my fortunes, I typed all my aphorisms into two narrow columns on a standard sheet of letter paper. Then I made a couple of dozen photocopies of this page and cut them up so that each aphorism was on its own rectangular strip. I stuffed these into an envelope and handed it to the man who always seemed to be standing in the doorway of Golden Gate Fortune Cookies smoking a cigarette. He, in turn, handed it to one of the two women. I then sat and watched as my fortune cookies were made.

Each woman sat before an enormous black iron wheel, which looked as if it had just fallen off a steam locomotive. The wheel, which rotated very slowly, was laid flat like a table and its circumference was stippled with small depressions about the size of a Petri dish. As each depression came into position under a thin metal funnel, a dollop of dough squirted into it. The wheel then entered what looked like a model

25

railway tunnel but was actually an oven, and by the time it emerged from the other side about thirty seconds later, the dough was baked into a miniature pancake, golden brown and steaming.

The women skewered each doughy medallion with a stick and lifted it from the wheel. Grabbing a fortune from a nearby tray, they swiftly inserted the aphorism into the soft, warm dough, deftly folded the cookie around it into its final croissant-like shape, and tossed it into a basket to cool. After about forty-five minutes, I walked away with a hundred of my own freshly baked fortune cookies, which I dropped into my trusty globe for distribution at the poetry performances I was giving at the time.

The origin of the fortune cookie is obscure. One theory holds that it is a variation on the moon cake, a sweetmeat filled with red bean paste. In the fourteenth century, when China was under siege from the Mongols, Chinese soldiers disguised as monks were said to pass messages to each other by secreting notes in moon cakes. Another theory says the fortune cookie is a more recent innovation: a marketing technique thought up by a Chinese entrepreneur to promote his restaurants. Whatever their true beginnings, fortune cookies are one of the few contemporary manifestations of 'wisdom writing', the ancient forerunner of the aphorism.

Wisdom writing is made up of terse, vatic statements that prescribe behaviour and give moral, practical or spiritual counsel. In the ancient world, these texts were extremely popular and circulated widely as far back as the second and third millennia BCE. Collections of wise sayings, often attributed to some legendary or mythical sage, were consulted for guidance on everything from the size of future harvests to the outcomes of impending battles. The Upanishads, Ecclesiastes and the Proverbs of Solomon are all classics of wisdom literature. But the earliest wisdom book, and perhaps the oldest book in existence, is the *I Ching*, the Chinese Book of Changes. It is with this ancient text that the history of the aphorism begins.

According to Chinese legend, the *I Ching* was compiled some five thousand years ago by the ruler and folk hero Fu Hsi. Originally intended as a method of divination, the Book of Changes embodies the essence of ancient Chinese philosophy: all is flux and everything is in the process of becoming something else. These transformations are chronicled in a cycle of sixty-four archetypal scenarios that cover the full spectrum of human life. Each scenario represents a primal experience, a situation everyone has faced or will face in the future. And since change is inevitable, each situation is shadowed by its opposite. The experience of 'Standstill', for example, is complemented by 'Progress', while 'Gathering Together' is paralleled by 'Splitting Apart'.

Each of the sixty-four scenarios is made up of six brief, aphoristic lines of text that both narrate and comment on the experience through a mix of blunt judgements and bewildering imagery. Specific sayings can be maddeningly obscure. It's difficult, for instance, to know what to make of the fourth line of 'Deliverance':

Deliver yourself from your great toe. Then the companion comes, and him you can trust.

27

But the book also has moments of intense poetic beauty, as in the fourth line of 'Enthusiasm':

Doubt not. You gather friends around you as a hair clasp gathers the hair.

Philosophers and scholars have puzzled over the *I Ching* for millennia. Today, many people still use the book for divination, turning to it for tips to ensure future success in their careers, love lives and friendships. In ancient times, readers wanting to consult the text did so by dividing up fifty yarrow stalks; today, they mostly do it by tossing three coins. For me, though, the real value of the book is not as a personal prognosticator. Like all wisdom writing, the *I Ching* has more to say about the here and now than it does about the future. The book's baffling, beguiling aphorisms challenge us to change, even as everything changes around us.

I regularly consulted the *I Ching* when I lived in San Francisco, not because I wanted a glimpse into my future but because I badly needed some perspective on my present. A failed relationship had dredged up a lot of really unpleasant stuff and I was stuck in a deep emotional rut. So I asked the *I Ching* for advice and got scenario number 48, 'The Well', in response.

On the surface, 'The Well' reads like an account of repairs to a municipal sewer system. The scenario describes a neglected well that has reverted to its wild state. Its lining is cracked and crumbling; the water is thick with debris and dirt. Line one states:

One does not drink the mud of the well.
No animals come to an old well.

But each of the next five lines details how the well is gradually cleaned out and repaired, until in line six it's once again a reliable source of clear, pure water:

One draws from the well
Without hindrance.
It is dependable.
Supreme good fortune.

Initially, I was flummoxed. What did a muddy old well have to do with my emotional crisis? Things cleared up only when I made the connection between this scenario and the symbol of Buddhist enlightenment, the lotus flower, which grows best in muddy ponds. The stem of the lotus is like a well, I thought. Rooted in the muck and slime on the bottom, it draws up dirty water, purifies it and uses it to feed its luxuriant blossoms. Then I understood what the *I Ching* was trying to tell me. I had struck bottom, too. I was wallowing in the mire of my emotional wounds and had allowed the clear, cold spring in my heart to become choked with some pretty nasty sediments. The thing to do was to use all that crap to nourish my roots – and get straight to work on the repairs.

My trip to the well is just one example of the way in which aphorisms clarify even the murkiest, most muddled minds. We all need to refresh ourselves from time to time at these ancient fonts. And occasionally, new sources bubble up, in the 1970s the artists Peter Schmidt and Brian Eno created *Oblique Strategies*, a set of some one hundred aphoristic playing cards. The deck is meant to be used like the *I Ching*. When confronted with an artistic or personal dilemma, pick a card and follow the instructions. One saying I find especially helpful is:

**Honour thy error as a hidden intention.**

Aphorisms are the original oracles. They evolved during a time when books were exceedingly rare and literacy was limited to a scholarly elite. Aphorisms thrived because they were accessible to everyone; their brevity, wit and imagery all made them fun to remember and impossible to forget. In the largely oral cultures of the ancient world, that made these types of wise sayings very popular. People became accustomed to walking around with their own little anthologies in their heads. That's why the sages, preachers and prophets who were the form's earliest practitioners used aphorisms to get their messages across. They knew that the wisdom of this writing was always timely, whether you're repairing an old well or cracking open a fortune cookie.

## Lao Tzu (*c.*604–531 BCE)
### How to Cook a Small Fish without Really Trying

It's impossible to say for sure whether Lao Tzu ever really existed. Legend has it that he was a historian of the Chou dynasty who was so fed up with the way the local aristocracy was running things that he decided to leave his home and his job to live alone in the mountains. On the way to his solitary retreat, Lao Tzu was stopped by a gatekeeper, who asked him to write down his teachings before departing. Like all ancient Chinese scholars, Lao Tzu was a student of the *I Ching*, so he adopted its homely aphoristic style for his own writing. The result is the *Tao te Ching*, a treatise covering everything you need to know about statesmanship, philosophy and personal virtue in eighty-one brief chapters.

That's more or less all there is to Lao Tzu's biography. No one knows what happened to him in the mountains, but the *Tao te Ching* became the primary scripture for Taoism, a quietist philosophy in ancient China which stressed the importance of living in accord with nature by aligning your mind with the Tao, which means 'path' or 'way'.

In Lao Tzu's time, China was ruled by a hereditary aristocracy that divided up the vast and unwieldy empire into small fiefdoms that were constantly at war with one another. Chaos dominated public affairs, so philosophers spent a great deal of time thinking about good governance, both personal and political. As a result, the lessons of the *Tao te Ching* apply at every level of human endeavour. The book can be read as an instruction manual on how to run your country, your business, your family or your life.

For aspiring politicians, Lao Tzu has this advice:

Ruling a large kingdom is like cooking a small fish; the less handled the better.

Cooking a small fish is extremely tricky. Poke and prod too much and the fish falls apart, tearing and flaking into little strips. The best strategy is to let the fish cook itself; flip it once or twice, but for the rest just let it sizzle till it's finished.

For Lao Tzu, the wise ruler is one who manages the process rather than the details of government. A leader who continuously pokes and prods into the minutiae of a big bureaucracy or a big business only stirs up trouble. He divides his attention in too many directions and so limits his effectiveness; he alienates his staff, who resent the micro-management; and he encourages complacency by conditioning people to expect the boss's divine intervention to solve every problem.

This advice is typical of Lao Tzu, who in the *Tao te Ching* repeatedly counsels that the best way to do good is to do nothing – or at least to do very little. This fundamental tenet of Taosim is known in Chinese as *wu-wei*, which is usually translated as 'non-action.' For cooks as well as kings, less is always more:

**The greatest carver does the least cutting.**

This aphorism contains a brilliant pun in Chinese since *chih*, the word that means 'to carve', also means 'to rule'. But Lao Tzu is not advocating laziness, nor is he shooing us down the path of least resistance. Far from it. Instead of 'non-action', a better interpretation of *wu-wei* might be 'not trying too hard', a type of exertion that can only be achieved by following the Tao.

What is the Tao? And how do you follow it without trying

32

too hard? If Lao Tzu had been quizzed on this, he would no doubt have responded like Louis Armstrong when asked to define jazz: 'If you have to ask, you'll never know.' I've been asking myself these questions since my fortune-cookie-making days in San Francisco, and years later I found an answer: following the Tao is like learning to ride a bicycle.

My two sons were eight and five years old respectively, and I was teaching them how to ride bikes. My younger son, Tristan, picked it up immediately. He's a determined, resolute guy, and once he sets his mind on something he's impossible to discourage. After I explained the basics of balancing, ped-alling and turning, and ran alongside him a few times, he was quickly off on his own, slapping my hand away from the back of the seat when I tried to steady the bike. He took a few wicked falls, but got right back up and in no time was racing around the block popping wheelies.

My elder son, Gilles, had a harder time. He's a bit cautious and fretful, and though he too acquired the basics very quickly, he was far more troubled by the falls. After taking a few tumbles, he threw his bike down in disgust, saying riding bikes was stupid and boring and he didn't want to learn it anyway.

After that, every session was the same. He would start off eager and excited but after the inevitable first crash he'd become worried, wanting to plan in advance what he would do if he encountered a gap in the pavement or a bumpy patch of grass. Soon he was so frustrated that every session ended with him kicking his bike and stomping off in disgust. It took several weeks, and lots of encouragement and argument, before Gilles finally overcame his fear of falling and found his balance. For me, few sights have been as delightful as that of those two boys hunched over their handlebars, pedalling furiously, whooping and hollering as they raced down the pavement.

Following the Tao and learning to ride a bike, I realized, are both mastered by instinct rather than deliberate thought.

Influenced by the *I Ching*, the Taoists believed that everything is in motion, nothing is permanent, and at some point everything becomes its opposite – day becomes night, summer becomes winter, failure follows success, old age succeeds youth. Whenever one state of affairs reaches its peak, another opposing state of affairs is already taking shape to replace it. Lao Tzu describes it like this:

He who stands on tiptoe does not stand firm;
He who takes the longest strides does not walk the fastest.

Wisdom, for the Taoists, consists in keeping your balance amid all this change, just as the cyclist remains upright by continuously adjusting to the terrain. You lean into the turns, pedal hard up the hills, coast down into the valleys. Just as Gilles couldn't learn to ride a bike by figuring everything out in advance, so the Tao can't be tamed by tactical forethought. You have to abandon yourself to it, trusting in your ability to roll with the punches and improvise.

This is not a recipe for philosophical passivity, though. The wise man accepts the evanescence of things and tries – but not too hard! – to anticipate change. We can't control events, but we know that nothing can remain the same for very long. So we should be prepared when the shift hits the fan. As Lao Tzu says:

Put [things] in order before they have got into confusion. For the tree big as a man's embrace began as a tiny sprout, the tower nine storeys high began with a heap of earth, the journey of a thousand leagues began with what was under the feet.

The great thing about following the Tao and learning to ride a bike is that once you've mastered them, you never forget.

## Buddha ($c.563$–$483$ BCE)
## Do-It-Yourself Enlightenment

Siddhartha Gautama, the man who became the Buddha, died at the age of eighty. As he lay on his deathbed, one of the final bits of advice he gave to his disciples was:

Be lamps unto yourselves.

These last words of the Buddha form the first principle of Buddhism.

As the son of a clan chieftain in the village of Lumbini, some 230 kilometres north of Benares in what is now Nepal, Siddhartha was born into a life of luxury, power and sensual pleasure. But as a young man he gave it all up to live as a mendicant, travelling from teacher to teacher, from one ascetic discipline to another, in pursuit of enlightenment. After six years of fruitless searching, he realized he would never find what he was looking for in the spiritual regimens of any guru. He needed to look inside himself. So he sat down under a tree, in a place now known as Bodh Gaya, and resolved not to move from

35

that spot until he had seen the light. It was here that Siddhartha Gautama became the Buddha, 'the enlightened one', a term derived from the Pali word *budh*, which means to be awake.

What the Buddha woke up to under that tree was the realization that the only constant source of illumination is inner light. After his experience at Bodh Gaya, the Buddha spent the next forty-five years of his life as an itinerant preacher in northern India. But he never presented his insights as divine revelation. Enlightenment didn't come by merely accepting what someone else told you, he insisted. Each seeker had to discover the truth for him- or herself. The first step and final destination of that quest is the realization that what keeps us in the dark or lights us up is all inside our heads:

We are what we think.

This is the opening line of the *Dhammapada*, a collection of the Buddha's aphorisms originally compiled in northern India in the third century BCE and written down in Sri Lanka some two centuries later. The Buddha was a great talker and storyteller but not a writer. Yet most of his parables and sermons have an aphoristic core that contains the seed of his teaching. As the Buddha's fame spread, and the number of his sermons increased, his disciples needed a way to preserve and codify their master's lessons. Fortunately for them, all they had to do was write down the aphorisms that had already been burned into their memories.

*Dhamma* means law or truth and *pada* means path, so the *Dhammapada* is a route to the truth, a kind of spiritual road map. The Buddha taught that if you let your imagination run away with you down this path, you're sure to get lost:

Your worst enemy cannot harm you as much as your own thoughts, unguarded. But once mastered, no one can help you as much.

The mind is like a gushing spring; thoughts boil and roil incessantly inside it. At any and every moment we're thinking about dozens of different things, from rising or falling interest rates to erotic fantasies, from closing an important business deal to planning a child's birthday party. We inevitably live to a large extent inside our heads. But this constant stream of consciousness has dangerous eddies and undertows that can pull us into places we do not want to go. These are the unguarded thoughts the Buddha warns against.

Imagine you've sent a sensitive e-mail to someone. Maybe it's a close friend to whom you've confessed something very personal. Maybe it's a colleague to whom you've made an important business proposal. There's no immediate response. A day goes by, then another, and still nothing. Why no answer? The mind rushes to fill the void with a torrent of speculation. You wonder whether your friend secretly hates your guts and is deleting all your e-mails unread. Or worse, he's read your very private message and is circulating it on the Web. You suspect your colleague thinks your proposal is crap but can't be bothered to click the reply button. Or worse, she's stolen the plan and is even now presenting it to the boss as her own idea.

Are these scenarios true or false? It's impossible to know. Your friend might hate your guts, or he might just be on

37

vacation. Your colleague could be purloining your big idea, or she might be pondering the proposal in order to give it a more considered response. The point is, your thoughts flow on regardless of the facts. The mind revels in conjecture. Where information is lacking, it will gladly fill in the gaps. And before you know it, you're so far down the track on some runaway train of thought that there's no chance of ever getting back.

The Buddha realized that thoughts create their own reality. That's why they're so powerful – and dangerous. But he also knew that the mind is too wild and recalcitrant to be funnelled into neat and orderly channels. Trying to consciously control your thoughts is like trying to install a tap on Niagara Falls. Forget about it. Instead, the Buddha just said no to the flow. He stepped out of the stream of consciousness to stand on firmer ground. If you sit on the river bank, the current of thought ripples by with its usual force, but you're no longer swept away by it. This is the essence of what the Buddha called 'non-attachment':

The wind cannot shake a mountain. Neither praise nor blame moves the wise man. Happiness or sorrow – whatever befalls you, walk on untouched, unattached.

The cause of suffering, as the Buddha saw it, is not thinking itself but clinging to our thoughts. All the trivial and essential things bobbing around in our consciousness – cash and careers, mobile phones and sports cars, houses and health clubs, family and friends, privileges and perks – ebb and flood according to their own rhythms. Wanting, enjoying and striving for these

38

things is not the problem; clinging to them at all costs is. If you're tied to your job, your pleasures and your possessions by a thousand little strings, you're bound to get jerked around.

Non-attachment does not mean renouncing all worldly goods and human relationships. But it does require putting a safe distance between you and your thoughts, finding a place to stand outside the cascade of hopes, fears and desires. Non-attachment means being able to lose your job and keep your self-esteem, to slash your budget and still feel like a million bucks, to lose a loved one but not your love of life. When the things you have drop away, as they always will, non-attachment ensures you don't go under with them:

It is not life and wealth and power which enslave men, but the cleaving to life and wealth and power.

It sounds easy, a kind of lazy man's guide to enlightenment, but it's not. A soldier once asked one of the Buddha's disciples to describe the master's teaching. 'Do good, avoid evil, and keep your mind pure,' the disciple replied. 'That's it?' the soldier asked. 'A five-year-old child knows that.' 'Maybe so,' the disciple said, 'but few men of eighty can practise it.'

## Confucius (551–479 BCE)
### Private Ethics as Public Good

Confucius formulated what is perhaps the most foolproof moral rule ever devised. When asked by a follower for a word that could serve as a principle to guide one's life, he replied:

39

Is not reciprocity such a word? What you do not want done to yourself, do not do to others.

This is such a lovely rule because – unlike the precept ascribed to Jesus, 'Do unto others as you would have them do unto you' – it's impossible to use it to programme or preach or proselytize. It's an expression of respect and tolerance for other customs and traditions, the only sure way to avert a clash of personalities or civilizations. And it comes from a man who during his own lifetime was mostly derided or ignored.

The son of a noble family fallen on hard times, Confucius was orphaned as a young boy. Too poor to afford a formal education, he taught himself the Chinese classics – especially the *I Ching*, on which he wrote an extensive commentary – and in his early twenties became a tutor to the sons of the local nobility. His brilliance was widely praised, but his relentless honesty and forthright manner made it hard for him to find a job as a minister at court, the usual career route for bright young men such as himself. Confucius suffered his career disappointments with equanimity, though. In fact, he made doing so one of the central tenets of his philosophy:

I am not concerned that I have no place, I am concerned how I may fit myself for one. I am not concerned that I am not known, I seek to be worthy to be known.

Though he never attained a government post, Confucius did attract a large and devoted following. These disciples, eager to amass their master's scattered teachings in one place, compiled the *Analects*, a record of Confucius's aphorisms and conversation. The *Analects* clearly show the influence of the *I Ching* on Confucius's thought; he emphasizes the same pragmatic wisdom as the ancient book of aphorisms he loved so much.

As an aspiring minister, Confucius was a total failure. But as a moral philosopher, he is unparalleled in Chinese history. Three centuries after Confucius's death, the teaching of the man who couldn't get a job at court became the official state philosophy.

But in Confucius's own time, the country was gripped by the same incompetence and corruption that Lao Tzu experienced. (Some sources say Confucius was a younger contemporary of Lao Tzu, and that the two men once met.) Feudal lords skirmished among themselves; government officials, who inherited their positions, pursued endless campaigns for conquest and personal enrichment; law and order broke down as barbarian hordes began picking off the most vulnerable fiefdoms. Despite all this – and as alien as it sounds to our own political culture – Confucius believed that politics was a branch of morality and that private ethics determined the public good:

When a country is well governed, poverty and a mean condition are things to be ashamed of. When a country is ill governed, riches and honours are things to be ashamed of.

Confucius despised the aristocracy – no wonder no court would employ him – and intended his philosophy to overturn their rapacious and venal brand of government. Wisdom and nobility are not inherited at birth, he said, but earned by individual effort. Ministers should be servants not masters of the people, tending them with the same loyalty and devotion as they would members of their own families. For Confucius, doing good means being good, the greatest virtue is sincerity, and the greatest sage makes the greatest leader:

He acts before he speaks, and afterwards speaks according to his actions.

When he was in his fifties, Confucius left his home and spent the next ten years wandering through China in search of a ruler who would put his ideas into practice. He travelled from court to court, from fiefdom to fiefdom, but never found one. It would be another three hundred years before China's leaders began to seek out his teachings. Despite the many rebuffs and disappointments, Confucius always practised what he preached, and his stubborn quest during the last years of his life is proof of one of his greatest aphorisms:

The commander of the forces of a large state may be carried off, but the will of even a common man cannot be taken from him.

## Jesus ($c.4$ BCE–33)
## The Master Builder

Jesus was a mischievous little boy. Walking into the marketplace one morning, he saw a group of kids playing with some clay pigeons. Bored by such childish games, Jesus transformed the clay figures into real pigeons and laughed as they flew from the hands of the astonished children. On another occasion, Jesus was helping Joseph in the carpentry shop when Joseph mistakenly cut a beam too short. Seeing his father's distress, Jesus gently tugged on the end of the beam, extending it until it reached the right length.

The young Jesus had a dark side, too. Conscious of his brilliance and his power, he was often rude to his father and dismissive of his teachers. He casually resurrected and interrogated corpses, once quizzing the rotting skull of the late king of Yemen. And he had a bit of a temper. When a boy accidentally bumped into him, he struck the unfortunate child down in a fit of anger. Jesus didn't hold a grudge, though. He later raised the boy from the dead, along with all the other people he had impetuously murdered.

You won't read any of these stories in the New Testament, of course. They are part of the Gnostic gospels, accounts of Jesus's life and teachings written around the same time as the canonical scriptures – the end of the first and beginning of the second century – but rejected as heretical by the early Church leaders. This other bible also contains alternative versions of some Old Testament myths, such as that of Genesis (creation was a mistake, and whoever said 'Let there be light' a buffoon) and our fall from grace in the Garden of Eden (Eve was right to eat the apple because knowledge is good). But the manuscripts were suppressed during the fourth century as the Church consolidated its power. If not for an accidental discovery by some Egyptian peasants, these ancient scriptures might have been lost for ever.

In 1945, two brothers were digging around the foot of Jabal al-Tarif, a steep cliff that flanks the Nile not far from the city of Nag Hammadi, in search of a naturally occurring fertilizer. As they rooted around in the dry, dusty soil, they uncovered a large earthen storage vessel which was sealed at the top. Thinking they had found a buried treasure, they smashed open the jar and stood amazed as a cloud of golden flakes swirled out – fragments of the 1,500-year-old papyrus scrolls inside. There were thirteen separate books in all, probably buried for safe-keeping around 400, which together are known as the Nag Hammadi library. The manuscripts include the stories from Jesus's childhood as well as the Gospel of Thomas, which records 114 of Jesus's most startling aphorisms.

My own discovery of the Gospel of Thomas took place in the Catholic secondary school I attended. In a class on the history of the early Church, I read about the Gnostics, who sought a direct relationship with God without the intervention of priests or sacraments and wrote many of the Nag Hammadi tracts. This sect stressed that enlightenment was achieved through gnosis, or spiritual self-knowledge. They believed an official church, with a clerical hierarchy and approved liturgy, prevented people from pursuing gnosis.

Naturally, this didn't go down well with early Church fathers such as Irenaeus who were at that time codifying Christian teaching. We read Irenaeus's invective against the Gnostics in class but none of the Gnostic scriptures. So I did a little digging of my own and found the Gospel of Thomas, which revealed to me a more eloquent, more radical Jesus than I had ever encountered:

Show me the stone that the builders rejected: that is the cornerstone.

In the New Testament, Jesus talks about the rock on which he will build his church. But in the Gospel of Thomas, he doesn't say anything about founding a church. He doesn't perform any miracles, institute any sacraments or die for anyone's sins, either. He simply speaks, and his words are clearly meant for the outsiders, the rebels and the sceptics who are uncomfortable with other people's spiritual blueprints. The real foundation, Jesus says, is the rejected stone, the one that can't be shaped to fit someone else's plan. And that was a message a teenage misfit such as myself could believe in.

The aphorisms in this little tract were clearly recorded by someone who appreciated their wisdom and wanted the sayings to speak for themselves, unclouded by the myth-making of the early Christian fathers or the institutional agenda of the young Church. For these reasons, the Gospel of Thomas is as close to Jesus in his own words as we're ever likely to get, which is why it, instead of the other gospels, is so important to the history of the aphorism.

In the Gospel of Thomas, Jesus is far more subversive than he is in the New Testament, but he's far more human, too. Sometimes, he can be downright banal. I imagine him sitting by the side of some lake, urging his disciples to bear their poverty with fortitude and stay focused on their inner quest. I can almost hear him sighing in exasperation as he says:

Do not worry, from morning to evening and from evening to morning, about what you will wear.

45

Many of the aphorisms in the Gospel of Thomas are similar to those in the New Testament. For example, this saying:

You see the speck that is in your brother's eye, but you do not see the beam that is in your own eye. When you take the beam out of your own eye, then you will see clearly to take the speck out of your brother's eye

is practically identical in both books. The author of the Gnostic text – said to have been Judas Thomas, Jesus's twin brother and disciple – was clearly using some of the same sources as Matthew, Mark, Luke and John. But even when the aphorisms share similar themes, the Jesus in the Gospel of Thomas goes well beyond the bounds of orthodoxy.

In Matthew's New Testament Gospel, Jesus speaks to a crowd about the kingdom of heaven, comparing it to a mustard seed, a net cast into the sea, a treasure buried in a field. He addresses the topic in Thomas, too, but in entirely different terms. He first warns his listeners to spurn any teaching that puts the kingdom out of reach in some faraway, inaccessible place. Then he tells them that the kingdom is near, and to find it they must enquire within:

If your leaders say to you, 'Look, the kingdom is in heaven,' then the birds of heaven will precede you. If they say to you, 'It is in the sea,' then the fish will precede you. Rather the kingdom is inside you and it is outside you. When you know yourselves, then you will be known, and you will understand that you are children of the living father.

46

The Jesus of the Gospel of Thomas is a sage rather than a saviour. He's very much a human being who wants to help other human beings find their own paths to gnosis. He professes a single article of faith: believe in yourself. Being the oddly shaped cornerstone of your own chapel is more difficult, but spiritually more rewarding, than being just another brick in the wall of someone else's cathedral:

Let one who seeks not stop seeking until one finds. When one finds, one will be troubled. When one is troubled, one will marvel and will rule over all.

## Muhammad (570–632)
### The Commerce of the Soul

Muhammad was napping one afternoon under a palm tree when he awoke with a start to see a man standing over him holding a sword to his throat. 'Who will save you now?' taunted the man, who had been sent to assassinate the Prophet. 'God,' Muhammad replied calmly. The would-be assassin was so disarmed by this response that he dropped his sword and fell to his knees. Muhammad swiftly stood up, grabbed the weapon, held it to the man's throat, and asked: 'Who will save *you* now?' 'No one,' the man answered. 'Then learn from me the art of mercy,' Muhammad said, and handed back his sword.

This story perfectly captures Muhammad's dual role as warrior and sage. He preached a benevolent morality based on

47

honesty, moderation, charity and – as his encounter with the assassin shows – forgiveness. He placed learning among the highest virtues:

The ink of the scholar is more holy than the blood of the martyr.

But Muhammad was a fighter, too. When the Meccan rulers in what is now Saudi Arabia resisted his message, he converted them to Islam by force.

Muhammad was an unlikely prophet. Born in Mecca, he was an illiterate camel driver who spent his youth and early manhood in the desert working the caravan trade routes between Yemen and the Levant. Then, when he was forty years old, he had a revelation as he rested in a cave on the slopes of Mount Hira.

He awoke from a nap to find himself in the vice-like embrace of the angel Gabriel. The angel held him so tightly that Muhammad felt as if the breath would be forced out of him. 'Recite!' Gabriel commanded. When Muhammad protested that he was illiterate, the angel steadily tightened his grip until the first verses of the Koran burst from Muhammad's lips. Muhammad had visions like this for the rest of his life, and his divine recitations were faithfully transcribed by his followers, who compiled a written form of the Koran around 650.

Muslims believe the Koran is the word of God. But the Hadith, a collection of aphorisms by and anecdotes about the Prophet, is Muhammad's own words of wisdom. He insisted that the Koran was divine dictation, but that his own sayings were just the thoughts of an ordinary man. And being illiterate himself, Muhammad chose the aphorism as the best way to get his extraordinary thoughts across.

In the roughly 1,500 aphorisms in the Hadith, Muhammad speaks as a practical prophet, someone with deep spiritual instincts who integrates his revelations with the more mundane concerns of daily life. He mixes faith with pragmatism, and a little hint of humour:

Trust in God, but tie your camel.

Many of Muhammad's aphorisms deal with the challenge of keeping a spiritual perspective in the midst of a busy secular life. After all, until his tussle with Gabriel, Muhammad was a businessman, concerned more with profits than with prophecy. His aphorisms retain a brisk, businesslike quality, and he often reverts to images from his trading days to illustrate his points:

Everyone starts the day selling his soul, and either frees it or ruins it.

Muhammad knew from personal experience that living is a risky business. People thought he was crazy when he talked about his sessions with the angel Gabriel, and he was ostracized from the community for his heterodox beliefs. Tribal leaders plotted against him, because his brand of monotheism clashed with the idolatry of the times and because they feared his strange new sect would threaten their control of the lucrative pilgrimage routes to the sacred city of Mecca. But instead of selling out, Muhammad persisted with his vision – and those who weren't persuaded by his words were persuaded by his sword.

Throughout his religious and military campaigns, Muhammad retained a resolutely practical approach to the soul's commerce. Life is a transaction between you and God, he thought, so make sure you spend your spiritual capital wisely. For him, there was no better investment than a little introspection:

An hour's contemplation is better than a year's adoration.

The illiterate camel driver never forgot that a smart investor can turn a little learning into a powerful thing:

Acquire knowledge. It enables its possessor to distinguish right from wrong; it lights the way to heaven; it is our friend in the desert, our society in solitude, our companion when friendless; it guides us to happiness; it sustains us in misery; it is an ornament among friends, and an armour against enemies.

## The Zen Masters (c.960–1279)
## The Sound of One Mind Flapping

The American baseball player Yogi Berra was a pretty good athlete, and not a bad head coach either, but few would place him in the pantheon of great thinkers. Off the baseball field, he's best known for his malapropisms rather than his insight into the deep philosophical questions of our time.

For example, it was miserably hot and humid on the day Yogi received the key to New York City. Standing on the platform waiting for the ceremony to begin, the mayor's wife turned to him and remarked how cool she thought he looked. 'You don't look so hot yourself,' was his reply. Or take his advice on attending funerals, given to a friend after reflecting on how many of their mutual acquaintances had recently passed away: 'Always go to other people's funerals; otherwise they won't go to yours.' Then there's the time in an Italian restaurant when he was asked whether he wanted his pizza cut into four or eight slices. 'Four,' he said. 'I don't think I can eat eight.'

Yet many of Yogi's sayings have deeper meanings. Just as tacky wallpaper can conceal a gorgeous mural, Yogi's seeming nonsense masks real wisdom. Take his most famous saying:

It's déjà vu all over again.

On the surface, this is an absurd tautology, a kind of philosophical faux pas. But if you think about it, the phrase is a miraculously apt expression of the exasperation we feel when some recurring personal foible gets us into trouble, when we fall for the wrong guy or girl again.

When asked the time, Yogi was in the habit of asking straight back: 'You mean now?' That's a ridiculous thing to say, of course, but it also has a whiff of mysticism about it, reminding us that there's no time like the present.

Yogi Berra's inadvertent aphorisms make sense in the same wacky way Zen koans do: by short-circuiting conventional meanings and circumventing our normal powers of reasoning.

The Japanese word *koan* (a term derived from the Chinese word *kung-an*, which originally meant a government file or document) is a literary form developed by Buddhist monks in China between the tenth and thirteenth centuries. Koans are aphorisms disguised as riddles and usually take the form of terse, witty dialogues between a Zen master and his students. They often involve some weird, irrational or slapstick element and – compiled into two great collections, the *Mumonkan* and the *Hekiganroku* – were used as bizarre case studies for aspiring monks.

A typical koan is the account of an exchange between a master and a student. Often the plot of these compact little stories goes something like this: seeking enlightenment, the monk asks a question and the master replies with some nonsensical remark, sometimes accompanied by a swift blow to the neck with a stick. A classic example is the koan 'A Sesame Bun':

A monk asked Ummon, 'What is the teaching that transcends the Buddha and patriarchs?' Ummon said, 'A sesame bun.'

The point of this koan – of any koan, in fact – is that there is no point. There is no right answer and no prize for coming up with something clever. Clinging to the words of your master, or even to the words of the Buddha himself, can only hold you back. Zen teaches you have to let go of even that. So koans were used as a kind of mental gymnastics to prepare students for the big leap beyond words. Only when the rug of logic and language was pulled out from under them would students understand how the mind works:

The wind was flapping a temple flag, and two monks started an argument. One said the flag moved, the other said the wind moved;

they argued back and forth but could not reach a conclusion. The Sixth Patriarch said, 'It is not the wind that moves, it is not the flag that moves; it is your mind that moves.' The two monks were awe-struck.

The Christian tradition has its koan collections, too. Back in the fourth century, when Irenaeus was busy defining orthodoxy and the Gnostics were burying their gospels on the banks of the Nile, small communities of monks inhabited the deserts of Egypt, Syria and Palestine. They lived simply and spent their time in meditation, supporting themselves by weaving baskets and mats from reeds and palm leaves. Like the Zen masters, they discouraged abstract, theological discussions but endured a steady stream of students and visitors looking for the one small word that would tip them into enlightenment. These encounters are preserved in the *Apophthegmata Patrum*, or Sayings of the Fathers. One classic account goes like this:

The same Abba Theophilus, the archbishop, came to Scetis one day. The brethren who were assembled said to Abba Pambo, 'Say something to the archbishop, so that he may be edified.' The old man said to them, 'If he is not edified by my silence, he will not be edified by my speech.'

The Zen masters and Christian monks employed nonsense and silence to turn the seeker's mind back upon itself. Their catechism lists all the right questions, but leaves blank the page where all the answers should be. As Benedicta Ward, who translated the *Apophthegmata Patrum*, says, the wisdom of

53

the desert fathers – and that of all the ancient aphorists – is 'not taught but caught'. These early aphorisms are fleet, elusive, ineffable. They come from strange times and often alien cultures. Yet once you catch their meaning, they are immediately familiar, like the sudden meeting of two long-lost friends. As Yogi Berra would say, it's like déjà vu all over again.

# 2 A man is wealthy in proportion to the things he can do without:

*Greek and Roman Stoics*

My wife's grandfather lived to the ripe old age of eighty-eight. Born into a wealthy Amsterdam family, he made his career in the insurance industry, but his first loves were art and music. He was an accomplished violinist, and as a young man in the 1930s lived the bohemian life in Paris, where he dedicated himself to painting. He was a sprightly, imperturbable optimist who loved good food, fine wine and lively company. He was what the Dutch call a *levensgenieter*, someone with a talent for enjoying life to its fullest, a real connoisseur of living. Even during his final days, his appetite for life never diminished. One of the last things he said was, 'I think it stinks that I'm dying.'

He had a maxim that he trotted out every time one of his friends or family members faced a disappointment or setback. 'It's a question of mind over matter,' he would say. 'If you don't mind, it doesn't matter.' That's not a bad summation of Stoic philosophy.

Stoicism was founded by Zeno, a Cypriot who came to

Athens between 320 and 315 BCE. His philosophical school took its name from the place in which he normally lectured: the *stoa*, or porch, an open colonnade that surrounded many ancient Greek buildings. Like Lao Tzu, Zeno lived during a time of general political and moral decline. The authority of the Greek city-state was waning, and the influence of religion and social mores was beginning to collapse along with it. So like the Taoists, the Stoics turned to nature as the only reliable model for morality and personal well-being.

Zeno broadly defined nature as 'the way things work', and wisdom meant acting in accordance with natural laws. For the Stoics, the first law of nature was: resistance to life's depredations – illness, ageing, poverty, grief and death – is futile. The smart thing to do, according to Zeno, was not deny these realities but find a way to live with them. So the second law was: because so much of what happens to you is outside your control, shift the focus to the one thing that is within your power – your attitude. In other words, happiness is a question of mind over matter.

The Stoic approach borrowed elements from the philosophies of two earlier Greek thinkers and aphorists: Heraclitus and Hippocrates. Pre-Socratic philosophers such as Heraclitus (540–480 BCE) examined the physical world to discover what it was made of, how it worked and where man's place was in it. Their goal was to identify the one immutable stuff from which the amazing variety of human experience emerged. Thales, for example, believed all things were water; Anaximenes thought air was the basic ingredient. For Heraclitus, the world was an 'ever-living fire' because, like a flame, it remained constant even while it was continually in flux. The only certainty was change, an observation Heraclitus expressed in one of his most famous aphorisms:

One cannot step twice into the same river, for the water in which you first stepped has flowed on.

The Greek physician Hippocrates was a prolific aphorist himself. He composed hundreds of terse, prosaic maxims around 400 BCE to instruct his students in the diagnosis and treatment of disease. Most of his sayings are straightforward tips on how to spot various illnesses or what it means when patients display specific symptoms. But he occasionally waxed philosophical, as in this reflection on the healer's task:

Life is short, and art long; the crisis fleeting; experience perilous, and decision difficult. The physician must not only be prepared to do what is right himself, but also to make the patient, the attendants and externals cooperate.

Like the sages, preachers and prophets who came before them, Heraclitus and Hippocrates used aphorisms as teaching tools. Unlike most of their ancient predecessors, though, the Greek and Roman Stoics deliberately set out to establish schools, and their collected sayings were intended to serve as both textbooks and instruction manuals. They wanted their words to be put to use, just as Hippocrates expected young physicians to regularly consult his medical maxims. The Stoics not only talked in aphorisms, they (or usually their students) also systematically wrote them down – in letters, lectures and private notebooks – and so gradually compiled a consistent body of doctrine. During this period, the aphorism gradually made the transition from spoken word to literary form.

The Stoics had one simple basic teaching: unhappiness results from an attitude problem; namely, the refusal to accept the way things work. The solution is to accept Hippocrates' diagnosis, acknowledging the brevity of life, the perils of experience and the difficulty of decision. Then mix in the Heraclitean dictum that change is inevitable, and add the realization that it's often impossible to coax external events into cooperating with our ideas of how things ought to be. The result is *ataraxia*, imperturbability, an inoculation against life's vicissitudes that works by building up our internal resistance.

The Stoics never claimed to offer a cure for the human condition. In fact, fatalism is a crucial part of their philosophy. Yes, there are good times as well as bad but neither prosperity nor happiness can last. Zeno and his followers did insist, though, that we can alleviate the worst symptoms by adopting the right attitude towards our afflictions. Concede the transience of pleasure and the inevitability of death; greet each fresh loss with poise and equanimity; and renew each day your determination not to let your happiness depend on anything but yourself.

The Stoics are the great physicians of the soul. Though their aphorisms often sound bleak, the message is a challenging yet hopeful one: reader, heal thyself.

## Diogenes (404–c.323 BCE)
### Mad, Bad and Dangerous to Know

Diogenes was the bad boy of ancient Greek philosophy. He made a great display of his disdain for the accoutrements of normal life. He slept outside in a tub, lived with a pack of stray dogs and relied on handouts for food and clothing. He had little regard for conventional morals. He famously went looking for an honest man and couldn't find one, even with a lamp in broad daylight. And he thought metaphysics was useless. The only worthwhile philosophy was one that helped people live a good life in the here and now. Francis Bacon, in the collection of ancient aphorisms and anecdotes he published in 1624, relates an encounter with Plato that captures Diogenes' provocative, pugnacious nature:

Plato entertained some of his friends at a dinner, and had in the chamber a bed, or couch, neatly and costly furnished. Diogenes came in, and got up on the bed, and trampled it, saying, 'I trample upon the pride of Plato.' Plato mildly answered, 'But with greater pride, Diogenes.'

Diogenes was a proto-Stoic. Though he died before Zeno's school was founded, he shared the Stoic view that the virtuous life was lived in harmony with the laws of nature. He believed the pursuit of wealth, fame and status was just a distraction. By so ostentatiously rejecting these customary measures of success, he sought to simplify his life, to free himself from the psychological slavery that keeps so many bound to an endless chain of ambitions and desires.

Diogenes ridiculed the Joneses instead of trying to keep up with them. Don't put in a sixty-hour working-week just so you can afford the latest fashion, he counselled. The pursuit of that kind of happiness is a race that can't be won, because the finish line recedes with every step. You cannot slip into the same dress twice because the trend of the moment has already flowed on. Diogenes' alternative:

To own nothing is the beginning of happiness.

Diogenes was well acquainted with the experience of owning nothing. Before arriving in Athens, he was captured at sea and sold into slavery. During the auction at which he was up for sale, Diogenes is said to have selected his future owner, a man called Xeniades, by pointing him out in the crowd and saying, 'Sell me to that man. He needs a master.'

Diogenes was as good as his word. Starting out as a household servant, he became tutor to Xeniades' sons and eventually came to be regarded as part of the family. He never wrote a book; his aphorisms were recorded by fellow Athenians who admired – or reviled – him. He was like a grubby, grumpy Confucius: even though many spurned his teachings, none could ignore his eloquence. As a result, a lot of his aphorisms survived. Diogenes' good fortune is emblematic of his belief that

The art of being a slave is to rule one's master.

60

The first task in this mastery is to throw off the shackles of convention. Diogenes was renowned for his impudence and crudity. He scorned the things the rest of the community held dear and rejected the values everyone else embraced. To him, good manners and etiquette were trivial and arbitrary:

Go about with your middle finger up and people will say you're daft; go about with your little finger out, and they will cultivate your acquaintance.

But his rudeness was not gratuitous. The obsession with possessions and politesse was incompatible with the virtuous life, Diogenes thought, because it blinded people to what really mattered – the search for values that endure beyond the latest fads. By shredding commonly accepted ideas of right thinking and polite behaviour, he ripped away the masks that shielded people from the need to ask uncomfortable questions about themselves.

Though he was wild, ill mannered and insolent, Diogenes had a lot in common with a much kinder, gentler philosopher – Socrates. Both men were subversive thinkers who made a point of rejecting received wisdom in public; both got their ideas across through lively argument rather than through abstract theory; and both thought the status quo was not worth preserving. The difference is that Diogenes used shock tactics to force people to examine their own behaviour, whereas Socrates used gentle but relentless persuasion. Yet Socrates would certainly have agreed with Diogenes' description of what he was doing:

If, as they say, I am only an ignorant man trying to be a philosopher, then that may be what a philosopher is.

The philosophers had one more thing in common. Both passionately believed that the unexamined life was not worth living.

## Epicurus ($c$.341–270 BCE)
### In Pursuit of the Pleasure Principle

In modern parlance, an epicure is someone with a highly refined palate who is especially fond of luxury and sensual pleasure. But this definition doesn't do justice to what Epicurus, from whom epicures take their name, actually taught. He was definitely no ascetic, believing that

Pleasure is the beginning and end of the blessed life.

And he wholeheartedly endorsed sensual delectation. But Epicurus also advised against indulging every whim and craving, warning that happiness was not achieved by conspicuous consumption but by paring down desires to a minimum:

A man is wealthy in proportion to the things he can do without.

So how do you live the blessed life while at the same time maximizing the number of things you can do without? Epicurus prescribed what might be called enlightened hedonism, an approach to pleasure that sought a happy medium between appetite and avarice, gratification and gluttony. Cupidity is the root of all evil, Epicurus believed, because it's insatiable, leading always on in an endless pursuit of the next sensation, leaving us always panting after some new titillation. The blessed life is lived in moderation.

To put his ideas into practice, Epicurus bought a big house with a large garden and set up his philosophical school there. Students lived together in a kind of socialist commune; money from the wealthiest members was redistributed among the poorest so that everybody's basic needs were taken care of. Epicurus himself was said to have had very simple tastes, living mostly on a diet of bread and cheese. Though he created his own little Eden, where he wrote his essays and aphorisms, Epicurus was careful not to let his students drift too far from the real world, encouraging them to work and manage their affairs outside the commune's walls.

Like Diogenes, Epicurus rejected metaphysics, instead taking a Hippocratic approach to philosophy. In his view, philosophers were psychological doctors tending the wounds inflicted by outrageous fortune:

Vain is the word of a philosopher, by which no mortal suffering is healed. Just as medicine confers no benefit if it does not drive away bodily disease, so is philosophy useless if it does not drive away the suffering of the mind.

Epicurus' diagnosis of the cause of suffering is remarkably similar to the Buddha's: clinging to desires. Let go of those desires, and you eliminate the suffering.

63

It's no wonder we've elided the less pleasurable parts of Epicurean philosophy. Nothing seems so out of step with contemporary consumer culture than eliminating desires. Shops are constantly flooded with new fragrances, new colours, new styles. We want our cars bigger, our phones smaller, our TV screens wider, our soft drinks super-sized. Our skin must be smoother, our stomachs flatter, our teeth whiter. There's no craving that can't be commodified. Indeed, the economy thrives on the multiplication of desires. So how do we cut down on the concupiscence?

Producing and consuming, buying and selling, getting and spending – these are necessary and beneficial economic pleasures, at least in moderation. Who doesn't enjoy splurging on a new dress, a better stereo system or a good meal in a fine restaurant? Indeed, Epicurus recognized that his garden of earthly delights would wither without the financial support of his wealthier students. There's no point in denying that money makes the world go round, or that consumption is key to spinning out economic growth. For Epicurus, the trick was to be in the whirl but not of it. To do that, you had to know one thing – when enough is enough:

Nothing is sufficient for the man to whom the sufficient is too little.

Sufficiency grants the longest-lasting pleasure. Gluttony is its own punishment. Burn the candle at both ends and you'll flame out; rack up too much credit-card debt and you'll wind up in bankruptcy court; eat too many cheeseburgers and you'll die of a heart attack; squander the earth's natural resources and the planet shrivels up.

The trouble with following Epicurus' teaching today is there's now so much stuff in the world that the bare necessities are easily lost in the excess. True epicures recognize the difference between what you need and what you want; jettison the non-essentials; remember that to be is not to buy. This is the way, Epicurus taught, to drive away the suffering of the mind and attain that blessed state in which

Self-sufficiency is the greatest of all wealth.

## Seneca ($c.4$ BCE–65)
## At the Vanishing Point

If, as Diogenes said, to own nothing is the beginning of happiness, Seneca must have been pretty miserable. He was among the richest men in Rome, having amassed a considerable fortune during his career as one of the most influential and eloquent speakers in the Senate.

Born in what is now Spain, Seneca won fame as a playwright and philosopher, but his impressive orations often got him into trouble. Emperor Caligula became so jealous that he ordered Seneca executed, a sentence that was later reversed. Emperor Claudius feared Seneca's powers of persuasion so much that he exiled him to Corsica. Despite the perils of Roman politics, Seneca managed to spend most of his life in that happy state John Lennon sang about – he could imagine no possessions, but he never actually had to experience it. So are we to take Seneca seriously when he writes:

65

You will only achieve [riches] in one way, by convincing yourself that you can live a happy life even without them, and by always regarding them as being on the point of vanishing.

Coming from such a wealthy man, this may sound like the worst kind of moral hypocrisy, a despicable case of philosophical dilettantism. But Seneca's life illustrates a key point of Stoic thought. Affluence itself doesn't automatically disqualify you from living the virtuous life; what matters is your attitude towards affluence.

The Stoics never encouraged anyone to take a vow of poverty, nor did they teach that money or personal possessions were a vice. Being rich or poor, famous or obscure, was irrelevant to the pursuit of virtue. The only thing that mattered was your disposition towards whatever good or ill fortune befell you. The fickle finger of fate can single you out for success one minute and hit the eject button the next. So Seneca's recipe for happiness was:

Do not regard as valuable anything that can be taken away.

This is a crucial piece of advice, because anything that can be taken away will be taken away: money, possessions, health, good looks, friends, family, even life itself.

This lesson was indelibly impressed on my mind one Christmas as my sons and I walked home from a matinée performance of *Peter Pan* at London's Royal Festival Hall. It was already dark when we came out of the theatre, a crisp, cold December afternoon. The kids crackled with Christmas excitement. We were crossing Waterloo Bridge, with the Thames unfurled below us like a necklace of lights, talking about how cool it would be to be able to fly like Peter Pan, when an elderly couple was struck by a car right in front of us.

The pair had tried to reach our side of the bridge by cutting across the busy lanes of traffic. They had almost made it to the pavement just in front of us when they were hit. There was a dull thud, and we saw their bodies tumble through the air, landing with a thump in the street, their limbs splayed like those of broken dolls.

We were horrified. My first thought was to rush the boys away, but that seemed pointless since it had happened right before our eyes and they had already seen the worst. We watched as people gathered around, calling the emergency services on their mobile phones. By the time we heard the first sirens, the man was sitting up, holding his head in his hands. The woman still wasn't moving. The boys took it all rather calmly, but as we resumed the walk to our car I realized I had a fist clenched tightly around each of their collars.

The experience left me shaken for days. What if my kids had run into the street and were hit? What if the car swerved to miss the elderly couple, leapt the kerb and struck my boys? It was a terrible reminder of how the things we value most are most vulnerable. This is the vanishing point Seneca talks about:

**Whatever can happen at any time can happen today.**

According to Seneca, the Stoic responds to life's fragility by being prepared for the worst even in the midst of the best:

Cling tooth and nail to the following rule: not to give in to adversity, never to trust prosperity, and always take full note of fortune's habit of behaving just as she pleases, treating her as if she were actually going to do everything it is in her power to do. Whatever you have been expecting for some time comes as less of a shock.

Seneca was in for a bit of a shock himself. He was recalled from his Corsican exile by Emperor Claudius's new wife, who appointed him tutor to her twelve-year-old son, Nero. When Claudius died, Seneca ruled for a time as regent until Nero came of age. But Seneca's adversaries turned the young emperor against him. In 65, a plot against Nero's life was uncovered and Seneca was said to be implicated. It was diplomatically suggested to him that he might like to take his own life.

He wasn't permitted to make a will, so in his farewell to his family Seneca said he would give them something more valuable than material wealth: the example of a virtuous life. Then he slit his wrists.

But he did not die quickly. His circulation was slow, so when his wrist wounds didn't do the trick he opened up the veins in his ankles and behind his knees as well. But still he did not die. He drank poison. When that failed to kill him he was placed in a vapour bath, where he eventually suffocated. Seneca's best epitaph is his own description of what he considered the proper Stoic attitude towards life – and death:

There is nothing the wise man does reluctantly. He escapes necessity because he wills what necessity is going to force on him.

This is Seneca's great philosophical pirouette. By accepting the inevitable, he suggests, we deprive death of its sting. Happiness does not consist in keeping what we've got but in enjoying it to the full even as it vanishes. The only way to beat fate is to refuse to fight:

It is in no man's power to have whatever he wants; but he has it in his power not to wish for what he hasn't got, and cheerfully make the most of the things that do come his way.

## Epictetus (*c.*55–*c.*135)
### To Have and To Have Not

We know Seneca's views on life and death thanks to the friendly and avuncular letters he wrote to the aspiring young philosopher Lucilius. But most of the Stoics wrote nothing at all. Their aphorisms survive only because they were recorded in the works of other authors or were meticulously written down by their students. For Epictetus, this service was provided by Arrian, a leading Roman citizen, politician and historian. 'I tried to note down whatever I heard [Epictetus] say, so far as possible in his own words, to preserve reminders for myself in future days of his cast of mind, and frankness of speech,' Arrian wrote in the preface to *The Discourses*, his account of Epictetus' talks.

Judging by Arrian's record, what Epictetus had to say was pretty straightforward. Like Seneca, he followed the standard Stoic line that we are not masters of our own fate, but must obey whatever the vagaries of life dictate. Unhappiness results when we hold mistaken beliefs about what falls within our sphere of influence. If we believe, for example, that we can control the value of our share portfolio, we're bound to be disappointed. For Epictetus, happiness increases in proportion to our ability to distinguish between what is and isn't under our control. He explained his differential wisdom like this:

The things that are up to us are by nature free, unhindered and unimpeded; the things that are not up to us are weak, enslaved, hindered, not our own. So remember, if you think that things that are naturally enslaved are free or that things not your own are your own, you will be thwarted, miserable and upset, and will blame both gods and men.

Echoes of this pragmatic philosophy can still be heard in the Serenity Prayer, which is recited before every meeting of Alcoholics Anonymous: 'God, grant me the serenity to accept the things I cannot change, courage to change the things I can, and wisdom to know the difference.'

Little is known of Epictetus' life, except that he was born in Hieropolis, now Pamukkale, in south-western Turkey, and that, like Diogenes, he was a slave who was eventually freed. He studied philosophy during Nero's reign and became a teacher, setting up his own school in Nicopolis, where Arrian was one of his most devoted students.

The only personal details known about him are that he married late in life, apparently to help raise an orphaned child, and was disabled. Some sources say his disability was the result of rheumatism, but others say it was caused by torture. The story goes that Epictetus' owner was punishing him by twisting his leg. Enduring the pain with typical Stoic composure, he warned that his leg was about to break. When it finally did snap, Epictetus quipped to his owner, 'I told you so.' He limped for the rest of his life.

The image of slavery recurs throughout Epictetus' lectures. I often think of him at the gym. Seeing everyone sweating on the running machines, hearing them grunting in the weight room, I wonder what he would have made of it. He wouldn't have objected to keeping fit, of course, but he specifically notes that our bodies are one of the things that we can't control. Yes, we can tone up muscles and gain or lose weight, but basically we're more or less stuck with the body we're born with. So what am I doing, huffing and puffing on the treadmill? If I'm chasing somebody else's idea of the perfect figure, or if I'm desperately pursuing my lost youth, then I really am just running in place – going nowhere fast. We enslave ourselves, Epictetus counsels, whenever we make our happiness dependent on something that's not within our power to achieve, whether that's the shape of our bodies or the trajectory of our careers:

A person's master is someone who has power over what he wants or does not want, either to obtain it or take it away. Whoever wants to be free, therefore, let him not want or avoid anything that is up to others. Otherwise he will necessarily be a slave.

There's a wonderful scene in the Buster Keaton film *Sherlock Jr* that is a kind of slapstick parallel to Epictetus' teachings. Keaton plays a cinema projectionist who secretly longs to be a

71

private detective. He falls asleep in the projection booth while screening a mystery – *Hearts and Pearls, or the Lounge Lizard's Lost Love* – and dreams that he enters the plot as a famous cinematic sleuth. In his dream, Keaton steps through the screen into the film to stand at the front door of a mansion. He knocks but no one answers. As he turns to leave, a rapid-fire montage of scene shifts abruptly occurs. Descending the front steps, Keaton finds himself in a garden just about to stroll off the end of a bench. Then he's in the middle of a busy street, on the edge of towering cliff, in a jungle staring into a lion's maw, stranded in a desert, perched on a rock in the ocean, stuck head first in a snowdrift and, finally, back in the garden again – all within the space of about sixty seconds.

For Epictetus, life is much like this Buster Keaton sequence, though usually not as funny. We continually find ourselves thrust into situations not of our own making, faced with a bewildering array of adversities. All the world's a stage, the director has just shouted 'Action!' and you haven't even read the script. The plot isn't up to us, Epictetus suggests, but the interpretation of your assigned role most certainly is:

What is yours is to play the assigned part well. But to choose it belongs to someone else.

## Marcus Aurelius (121–180)
The Last Stoic

The Stoics were equal-opportunity philosophers; their ideas applied equally well to slaves such as Diogenes and Epictetus,

72

to senators such as Seneca, and to emperors such as Marcus Aurelius.

Marcus Aurelius was born into a distinguished Roman family and became a favourite of Emperor Hadrian, who arranged for his own adopted heir, Antoninus Pius, to adopt Marcus Aurelius, thus placing him in the imperial succession. When Marcus came to the throne in 161, the empire was besieged by constant threats on the frontier. So as emperor, he spent most of his career quelling revolts and fighting back invading hordes. It was in the midst of these military campaigns that he wrote his *Meditations*, the candid and confessional journal that contains his aphoristic reflections on being a man, an emperor and a Stoic.

Hadrian called Marcus 'Verissimus', the most sincere of men, and the *Meditations* prove that an apt moniker. He writes very little about his military campaigns. Instead, his aphorisms record the battles he was fighting with himself – to see things clearly in the fog of war, to remain fair and just both on the battlefield and off, to apply the principles of Stoicism in his daily life.

The *Meditations* are in many ways restatements of the key principles of Stoicism, almost as if Marcus were rehearsing in his head the best Stoic aphorisms he had read. His reflections are like philosophical Post-it notes, quick reminders to put these principles into daily practice. Here is Marcus on the Heraclitean idea of constant change:

Repeatedly dwell on the swiftness of the passage and departure of things that are and of things that come to be. For substance is like a river in perpetual flux.

Here is his version of Seneca's admonition to seize the day:

Do each act as though it were your last, freed from every random aim, from wilful turning away from the directing Reason, from pretence, self-love and displeasure with what is allotted to you.

Marcus Aurelius was a real philosopher-king. But in his *Meditations* he also shows himself to be just an ordinary guy, living proof of the Stoic conviction that externals such as position, riches and fame ultimately don't matter. Not even a Roman emperor controls his own fate. We're all subject to the same trials and tribulations, the same doubts and depredations. What counts is character, how we respond to the necessities fate forces on us. As Marcus Aurelius puts it:

Every man is worth just so much as the worth of what he has set his heart upon.

# 3 Upon the highest throne in the world, we are seated, still, upon our arses:

*French and Spanish Moralists*

Know thyself. This admonition was inscribed above the doors of the temple at Delphi. But who said it first?

Ovid cites Pythagoras as the author of the rule. Socrates said Apollo himself thought it up. Diogenes Laertius ascribes it to Thales, who when asked 'What is difficult?' replied, 'To know oneself.' (When asked 'What is easy?' he said, 'To give another man good advice.') A character in one of Menander's comedies didn't care who said it. He thought the maxim was nonsense: '*Know thyself* in many ways is wrong; Far better were it, other men to know.'

We know so much about the possible provenance of this proverb because in 1500 Erasmus published a 152-page book called *Collectanea, A Collection of Paroemiae or Adages, Old and Most Celebrated, Made by Desyderius Herasmus Roterdamus, a Work both New and Wonderfully Useful for Conferring Beauty and Distinction on All Kinds of Speech and Writing*. It was the medieval equivalent of *Reader's Digest*'s 'Quotable Quotes', and it was an instant success.

Erasmus was an avid collector of proverbs and aphorisms. He compiled all the expressions he could find in the works of the classical Greek and Latin authors he loved, and provided a brief history and explication for each one. 'When I considered the important contribution made to elegance and richness of style by brilliant aphorisms, apt metaphors, proverbs, and similar figures of speech, I made up my mind to collect the largest possible supply of such things,' he wrote. So in addition to 'Know thyself', readers of Erasmus's *Adages* are treated to pithy accounts of the origins of such expressions as 'to leave no stone unturned', 'to cry crocodile tears', 'no sooner said than done', 'clothes make the man', and 'everyone thinks his own fart smells sweet'. Erasmus added to and revised the book throughout his life, and by the time he died in 1536 he had collected and explained 4,151 proverbs.

Erasmus intended the book to be an *Oxford Dictionary of Quotations* for sixteenth-century after-dinner speakers: a resource for writers and public orators who wanted to spice up their speeches with well-placed quotes from the classics. Erasmus's own writings are filled with these kinds of citations, and in compiling the *Collectanea* he was following the tradition of medieval florilegia, collections of the most beautiful *flores*, or flowers, plucked from the texts of other writers. These sayings were organized under individual categories for easy reference, just as anthologies of quotations are today. A writer in need of a quote could then look one up under the appropriate topic. During the Renaissance, these florilegia evolved into commonplace books – personal compilations of memorable thoughts, anecdotes, proverbs and aphorisms which are the distant ancestors of the modern pocket diaries and calendars filled with inspirational sayings which can be found today for sale near cash registers in gift shops and supermarkets.

The popularity of the *Adages* led to numerous reprintings, and in the 1508 edition Erasmus added an introduction in which he tried to define the proverb and describe both its beauty and its usefulness. Proverbs have been preserved through the ages, he wrote, 'partly because of their brevity and conciseness, partly owing to their good humour and gaiety'. And they are valuable, he believed, because they're the best method of inserting new thoughts into people's heads: 'An idea launched like a javelin in proverbial form strikes with sharper point on the hearer's mind and leaves implanted barbs for meditation.'

Erasmus's javelin, like Schlegel's porcupine, is an apt metaphor for the aphorisms of the French and Spanish moralists who lived between the sixteenth and eighteenth centuries. These writers obeyed the Delphic oracle's command with a unique thoroughness and fervour: they examined and analysed themselves, believing that to know their own minds was to know the minds of others as well. They were moralists, but not moralizers in the sense we understand the term today – preachy prescribers of right and wrong. Rather than condemn or condone behaviour, these authors simply tried to understand it, to expose human nature's highlights and lowlifes, to reveal our true and often hidden motives, and to try to discover an honest and honourable way of life. Striking deep, their verbal darts still leave plenty of implanted barbs

77

for meditation. The poignancy of their observations and the accuracy of their wit made this period the golden age of the aphorism in Europe.

## Michel de Montaigne (1533–92)
### The Unpremeditated Philosopher

Montaigne was thirty-eight when he began composing the *Essays*, his homely reflections on life and literature. He had already studied to be a lawyer and served thirteen years as a magistrate in the Bordeaux parliament. But he was tired of the intrigues of law and politics, occupations he never relished in the first place, and was still in mourning for the death of his close friend Étienne de la Boétie, who died suddenly of an intestinal complaint at the age of thirty-two. Montaigne was exhausted, depressed and dissatisfied. He wanted out.

So he quit his seat in parliament and retired to his ancestral home, a stern medieval chateau perched on a wooded hillside surrounded by vineyards above the banks of the Dordogne, about 30 miles east of Bordeaux. He commemorated his retirement in a Latin inscription painted on a wall of the old fortified tower he made into his chapel, bedroom and study. Though the wall has become severely dilapidated over the years, several phrases of that record are still legible:

In the year of Christ 1571, at the age of thirty-eight, on the last day of February, anniversary of his birth, Michel de Montaigne, long weary of the servitude of the court and of public employments, while still entire, retired to the bosom of the learned Virgins, where in calm and freedom from all cares he will spend what little remains of his life now more than half run out. If the fates permit he will complete this abode, this sweet ancestral retreat; and he has consecrated it to his freedom, tranquillity, and leisure.

What Montaigne planned to do with his new-found leisure was write. But it was no devout tome like those of his contemporaries that he intended to compose. He wanted to write something completely new and different, the first book of its kind in the world. 'Finding myself quite empty, with nothing to write about, I offered my self to myself as theme and subject matter,' is how he described this new literary venture in one of his *Essays*.

This was an unlikely pursuit for a man who until this point was known more as a doer than a thinker. By his own account, Montaigne was restless, garrulous and extroverted. He had a short attention span and a profound aversion to routine. He liked to socialize and take long, invigorating rides in the countryside. Why would a man like that want to hole up in his study to write, of all things, a book about himself?

The reason will sound familiar to us. Montaigne suddenly downshifted into philosophical mode in 1571 for the same reason that many people contemplate a career change as they approach their forties: a midlife crisis. He was severely shaken by la Boétie's death, and the shock of that tragedy forced him to rethink his priorities, to question what he was doing with his life.

But Montaigne's crisis was not just his own; it was all of Western civilization's. Montaigne lived at a time when the last vestiges of medieval thought were passing away. As old theological and ethical certainties waned, Renaissance and Enlightenment thinkers sought new truths in their own minds rather than in divine revelation. Montaigne was the first to emerge from the crisis of the Middle Ages and place himself at the centre of that quest. 'I study myself more than any other subject. That is my metaphysics; that is my physics,' he wrote.

After Montaigne, 'finding yourself' became a legitimate philosophical pursuit. As a result, he is the hinge between the ancient and modern worlds, between the Greek and Roman classics and today's memoirists and confessional poets. He was the first to interpret the ancient dictum 'Know thyself' as meaning 'Write thy autobiography'.

Montaigne called himself an 'unpremeditated philosopher', a man who combined scholarship with earthy wisdom. He was steeped in the classics as a child. His father insisted that his son hear nothing but Latin spoken in the family home, and to aid his mental development had the boy awakened each morning by chamber music. But as an adult Montaigne put all that learning to a peculiarly personal use. He sought answers to the age-old riddles – Who am I? What do I know? What should I do? – in himself and his own experiences.

Ironically for such an unpretentious man, Montaigne spent most of his time in an ivory tower. He made the chateau's round fourteenth-century tower his refuge, his library and his place of worship. When he left Bordeaux, Montaigne had the tower refurbished, creating a separate living and work space where he could find solitude, away from the business of running his estate and the cares of family life. The ground floor consisted of a small chapel, a simple altar with a painting of St Michel slaying the dragon behind it. (In English lore, St George performs this service.) Above the chapel was the bedroom, in which Montaigne carved out an acoustic passage leading to the chapel so he could hear mass when he was confined to bed by the pain of his kidney stones.

Above the bedroom was Montaigne's study. It contained a writing desk and a semicircular bookcase that ran along the length of the wall. Here he kept all his books, many of which he inherited after la Boétie's death. Like Erasmus, Montaigne was an aphorism collector and he found a novel way to display his favourites. On the bare wooden beams of the ceiling, he inscribed fifty-four aphorisms from classical and early Christian authors such as Euripides, Lucretius, St Paul, Pliny, Socrates and Sophocles, among others. These Latin and Greek inscriptions are still legible in Montaigne's study, though they were written there more than four hundred years ago. In several places it's clear where Montaigne rubbed out one aphorism and replaced it with another. The faint trace of the original is still legible underneath. Some of the inscriptions include:

I am a man; I consider nothing foreign to me. – *Terence*

I stop – I examine – I do not understand – I remain poised in the balance – I take for my guide the ways of the world and the experiences of the senses. – *Sextus Empiricus*

What upsets people is not things themselves but their judgements about things. – *Epictetus*

But by far the most citations, thirteen, come from Ecclesiastes, Montaigne's favourite book of the Bible, including this dark refrain:

All is vanity.

In his *Essays*, Montaigne delved into philosophical problems through the details of his personal life. He describes with equal verve and virtuosity both his morning ablutions and his defecations. We hear about his kidney stones, his sex life, his fondness for scratching, the virtues and faults of his friends, as well as his own peccadilloes.

Montaigne was a shrewd and practical man. Thirteen years as a magistrate exposed him to the best and worst in people. His patch of southern France was riven by religious wars between Catholics and Protestants in the sixteenth century, so he saw first hand the destruction wrought by those who believe God is on their side. As a result, Montaigne became a radical sceptic. 'What do I know?' was his motto. He lost faith in divine revelation and instead sought answers to big questions in little things:

I want Death to find me planting my cabbages.

Montaigne was a sixteenth-century Stoic, a kind of French Seneca relating the insights and experiences that helped him learn to live wisely in this world rather than the next. Like his ancient counterparts, Montaigne understood that a person can master events by mastering his or her attitude towards them:

The man who is happy is not he who is believed to be so but he who believes he is so.

He praised self-knowledge and sincerity as the highest virtues:

Truth for us nowadays is not what is, but what others can be brought to accept.

This last aphorism is particularly apt. We've grown so accustomed to businessmen, spin doctors and politicians being 'economical with the truth' that it often seems that we can be brought to accept just about anything. Cut the crap, would have been Montaigne's response. Forthright expression was everything to him. That's why his *Essays* are so revealing, and so appealing. In his view, to dissemble, deceive or feign was the gravest sin. He believed that real men and women do not lie, and neither do they spin:

Our understanding is conducted solely by means of the word: anyone who falsifies it betrays public society. It is the only tool by which we communicate our wishes and our thoughts; it is our soul's interpreter: if we lack that, we can no longer hold together; we can no longer know each other. When words deceive us, it breaks all intercourse and loosens the bonds of our polity.

In French, the meaning of 'essay' (*essai*) is 'an attempt'. Montaigne tried to understand his own, and mankind's, place in the world by looking inside himself, and then he tried to put that understanding into words. His *Essays* do not represent a

83

final answer to the question: What do I know? He was too much of a sceptic to believe that a final answer was possible, or even desirable. For him the pleasure was in the attempt at an answer rather than in the final result, which perhaps explains why he was constantly amending and revising the *Essays* – and why the book is more than 1,200 pages long! The aphorisms embedded in Montaigne's *Essays* are an exhilarating mix of the sublime, the mundane and the ridiculous, a bracing reminder that:

Upon the highest throne in the world, we are seated, still, upon our arses.

## Baltasar Gracián (1601–58)
## Machiavelli in the Monastery

Here's an unlikely aphorism to come from the pen of a Jesuit monk:

Life is a warfare against the malice of others.

Yet this is one of the central themes in *The Art of Worldly Wisdom*, a collection of sayings published in 1647 by Baltasar Gracián, who entered the Society of Jesus when he was eighteen. Gracián's crisp and crackling aphorisms apply equally well to spiritual seekers looking for enlightenment, social climbers trying to get ahead of the competition and harried middle managers determined to triumph in office politics. The book is all the more remarkable because, as a Jesuit, Gracián presumably had little direct experience of the worldly wisdom about which he wrote.

Born in the village of Belmonte near Calatayud in central Spain, Gracián was earmarked for the Church at an early age by his father. He was educated at the university in Toledo, where he was befriended by Vincencio Juan de Lastanosa, a sophisticated nobleman with a flair for epigrams. Lastanosa had his own art gallery and science museum and presided over a literary salon in the nearby town of Huesca. Gracián became a regular there and began to publish books: first *El Héroe*, a disquisition on the qualities of the ideal leader, and then *El Criticón*, an allegorical novel that criticized and parodied some of his contemporaries, including a few fellow Jesuits. Gracián used the royalties from these titles to start a collection of books and coins.

The Society of Jesus was less than pleased with the secular tone and subject matter of these works, to say nothing of the criticism of its own members. Retribution was swift. Gracián was denounced for publishing frivolous books unworthy of a priest. His penchant for collecting was condemned as a violation of the vow of poverty, and he was sentenced to a fast of bread and water as penance. He was kept under surveillance, his rooms were searched and he wasn't permitted to keep anything under lock and key. He could even be deprived of pen and ink, if necessary. Gracián, as it turns out, did know something about the 'malice of others'.

None of this stopped him from publishing *The Art of Worldly Wisdom*. The original Spanish title – *Oráculo Manual y Arte de Prudencia* – is more accurate because the book, a compendium of the best aphorisms from Gracián's earlier works, is indeed an oracle. Like the *I Ching*, it can be consulted for advice on everything from how to avoid answering awkward questions to the importance of anticipating trouble before it starts. The 300 aphorisms in *The Art of Worldly Wisdom* are like Montaigne's *Essays* in miniature. Gracián practised the long-form aphorism, or *pensée*, which is more wordy than the shorter version but no less pointed.

Gracián's book is part of a long tradition of leadership manuals which began, like the aphorism itself, with the ancient Chinese. *The Art of War*, written by the Taoist warrior-philosopher Sun Tzu more than two thousand years ago, was originally composed as a guide to victory in battle, but today is studied mostly by businessmen and politicians for its advice on how to vanquish opponents. *The Just Prince*, written by the Sicilian-born Arab thinker Muhammad ibn Zafar al-Siqilli in the twelfth century, is an Islamic counterpart to Machiavelli's *The Prince*, in which the author imparts tips to troubled rulers through elaborate moral fables. And the *Maxims and Reflections* of the sixteenth-century Italian historian Francesco Guicciardini are filled with pointers for success in public as well as private life. Though Gracián's concerns are more quotidian than those of his predecessors, his aphorisms are no less brilliant.

Looking to get ahead at the office but afraid of alienating the boss?

Avoid outshining your superiors. All victories breed hate, and that over your superior is foolish or fatal. Pre-eminence is always detested, especially over those in high positions. Caution can gloss over

86

common advantages. For example, good looks may be cloaked by careless attire. There are some that will grant you superiority in good luck or good temper, but none in good sense, least of all a prince – for good sense is a royal prerogative and any claim of superiority in that is a crime against majesty. They are princes, and wish to be so in that most princely of qualities. They will allow someone to help them but not to surpass them. So make any advice given to them appear like a recollection of something they have only forgotten rather than as a guide to something they cannot find. The stars teach us this finesse with happy tact: though they are his children and brilliant like him, they never rival the brilliance of the sun.

Contemplating a career in politics?

Know how to use evasion. That is how smart people get out of difficulties. They extricate themselves from the most intricate labyrinth by some witty application of a bright remark. They get out of a serious contention by an airy nothing or by raising a smile. Most of the great leaders are well grounded in this art. When you have to refuse something, often the most courteous way is to just change the subject. And sometimes it proves the highest understanding to act like you do not understand.

Need some encouragement to stick with a daunting task?

Attempt easy tasks as if they were difficult and difficult as if they were easy. In the one case so that confidence may not fall asleep, in the other so that it may not be dismayed. For a thing to remain undone nothing more is needed than to think it done.

87

Gracián's aphorisms are a curious mixture of virtue and guile. He's cunning but never cruel, calculating but not malicious. His intent is laudable – instructing people on how to live a good and successful life – yet in advising on how to get ahead he's not above recommending morally questionable short cuts or exploiting other people's weaknesses.

In fact, Gracián has a lot in common with that singularly unholy strategist Niccolo Machiavelli (1469–1527), whose cruelly pragmatic advice to rulers is expounded in *The Prince*. Though their callings in life couldn't have been more different, Gracián and Machiavelli share many of the same themes: how to exploit your advantages, how to exert and maintain control over people and situations, how to use other people's faults against them, when to attack and when to retreat. Many of their sayings are remarkably similar, too, and it's often startling to read how the cloistered musings of a Jesuit priest and the crafty stratagems of a ruthless courtier could offer the same conclusions.

Of dependence, for example, Gracián writes:

Make people depend on you. It is not he that adorns but he that adores that makes a divinity. The wise person would rather see others needing him than thanking him. To keep them on the threshold of hope is diplomatic, to trust to their gratitude is boorish; hope has a good memory, gratitude a bad one. More is to be got from dependence than from courtesy. He that has satisfied his thirst turns his back on the well, and the orange once squeezed falls from the golden platter into the waste basket.

And Machiavelli writes:

A wise prince must devise ways by which his citizens are always and in all circumstances dependent on him and on his authority; and then they will always be faithful to him.

On meting out rewards and punishments, Gracián advises:

Do pleasant things yourself, unpleasant things through others.

And Machiavelli agrees:

Princes should delegate to others the enactment of unpopular measures and keep in their own hands the means of winning favours.

On destroying your enemies, Gracián counsels:

Push advantages. Strike down your quarry, if you are wise – do not be content merely to flush it out.

And Machiavelli concurs:

Violence must be inflicted once for all; people will then forget what it tastes like and so be less resentful. Benefits must be conferred gradually; and in that way they will taste better.

Machiavelli's stratagems were designed to help aspiring despots grab and hold power, but Gracián had other motives.

89

His oracle was meant as a how-to manual for heroes. Gracián's ideal hero was no pumped-up action figure, though. Unlike Machiavelli, Gracián never writes about wars between states. Instead, he dwells on the daily domestic struggles between an individual and his colleagues, friends or himself. And Gracián has very little to say about grand affairs of state. He focuses solely on the home front, the psychological trenches where our personality clashes and battles of will take place.

So Gracián's hero is not someone who excels at intrigue or displays conspicuous valour on the battlefield, but someone who's modest, sincere, savvy and persistent:

Be slow and sure. Things are done quickly enough if done well. If just quickly done they can be quickly undone. To last an eternity requires an eternity of preparation.

For Gracián, it's the everyday contests which are heroic: the little battles we all fight to stay focused and do our best, to overcome our doubts and fears, to keep our cool when all about us may be losing theirs. Victory doesn't mean power and plaudits but a sense of fulfilment and self-respect. Machiavelli helps us defend against the malice of others, but to truly master the art of worldly wisdom the real hero must win a much more inward struggle:

First be master over yourself if you would be master over others.

## François, Duc de La Rochefoucauld (1613–80)
## The Soul Dissected

La Rochefoucauld was a broken and bitter middle-aged man when he began writing maxims in the 1650s. In his youth, he had been a wealthy and influential courtier. But he emerged a big loser from the series of civil wars known as the Fronde, an absurd period of French history during which constantly shifting alliances of noblemen fought a succession of pointless battles with the Crown for the restoration of their privileges and powers.

Royalty eventually prevailed, and La Rochefoucauld paid a heavy price for his insurgency. He was financially ruined, his family was driven from their ancestral home, and his other properties were seized and ransacked. His career prospects were obliterated, he was stripped of his titles and banished from Paris. He was a physical wreck, he'd been badly wounded in battle, nearly lost his eyesight and never fully recovered his health. And he was betrayed by his erstwhile allies, who in the disarray that followed their defeat displayed all the constancy of Afghan warlords. His only comfort was the fact that his partners in crime were punished just as severely, an observation that no doubt inspired one of La Rochefoucauld's most famous and cynical remarks:

**In the adversity of even our best friends we always find something not wholly displeasing.**

This was a remarkable reversal of fortune for François, Duc de La Rochefoucauld. Born in Paris, eldest son of the fifth

91

Count François of the ancient line of La Rochefoucauld, one of the noblest families in France, the young duke was a swashbuckling rogue fired by romantic ideals of heroism and gallantry. Like most men of his class he entered the military, but never really distinguished himself as a soldier. He excelled, however, in skulduggery and quickly became embroiled in court intrigue. He bore secret messages from Queen Anne to her various confidantes and lovers, and easily mixed affairs of state with affairs of the heart. He was suave, witty and ambitious, a born plotter. But he was also strangely irresolute, prone to melancholy and possessed of an uncanny ability to pick the losing side in any battle.

After the debacle of the Fronde, La Rochefoucauld retired to a relative's country estate, where he read Seneca and the other Greek and Roman Stoics. In 1656, the king permitted him to return to Paris but La Rochefoucauld's scheming days were over. The Stoics may have consoled him for the painful realization that all his mad pursuits and machinations had come to naught, that his youthful ideals of romance, honour and glory were a sham. Though still in his early forties, La Rochefoucauld was battered and beaten enough to speak from experience when he wrote:

Old people are fond of giving good advice; it consoles them for no longer being capable of setting a bad example.

In Paris, the horror and venality of the Fronde were replaced by the artifice and sophistication of the salon. In the late 1650s, it seemed no woman of rank and substance was without her

92

own salon, regular evening meetings during which a small group of intimate friends gathered to discuss life, love and literature. (Politics and religion were forbidden as too divisive.) Guests passed the time listening to music and playing literary parlour games that included impromptu verse competitions and the quick composition of brief verbal portraits, known as 'characters'. Grace, wit and exactness of expression were all the rage, so participants honed and shaped their observations into concise and elegant statements. One of the most famous of the Parisian salons was that of Madeleine de Souvré, Marquise de Sablé – and La Rochefoucauld was its star.

Madame de Sablé had two great loves in life: fine food and fine literature. At her salon, guests amply partook of both. She was intelligent, well read, an excellent cook, a minor aphorist, and a devotee of Jansenism, a Catholic fundamentalist sect that emphasized mankind's depravity, a faith she embraced after her lover was killed in a duel. (The scientist and inventor Blaise Pascal, another accomplished French aphorist, was a Jansenist too. Madame de Sablé became his spiritual confidante and he frequented her salon for a time.) But the great lady was not without her eccentricities. She had a pathological fear of infection, so the porter inspected salon guests as they arrived. If he noticed any coughs, sniffles or suspicious dermatological problems, they were turned away at the door.

La Rochefoucauld and Madame de Sablé became close friends, and he came to rely on her conversation and criticism during the composition of his aphorisms. The preparatory work for La Rochefoucauld's *Maxims*, his collection of terse and mordant sayings, was done in the convivial and collaborative

93

company of the salon. A topic – say, the fickleness of romantic love – was thrown out into the group, where it was discussed and dissected. Thoughts and opinions on the subject were bandied back and forth, scrutinized, refined and modified. La Rochefoucauld then withdrew to write, often beginning with a lengthy paragraph that he meticulously whittled down until only the essence survived. If Madame de Sablé approved, he had a fresh maxim to unveil at the next meeting of the salon:

In their first affairs women are in love with their lover, later they are in love with love.

*Amour* – or more accurately, *amour-propre* (self-love) – became the touchstone and subtext for all La Rochefoucauld's maxims. His experience of and involvement with the conniving cabals at court convinced him that all was indeed vanity, that the actions of men and women were motivated solely by their own advantage and self-interest:

Self-love is love of oneself and of all things in terms of oneself; it makes men worshippers of themselves and would make them tyrants over others if fortune gave them the means.

For La Rochefoucauld, fortune gave people the means to make themselves tyrants every day in all the little personal encounters and transactions they negotiated at home, at work and at play. Gracián's struggle against the malice of others became for La Rochefoucauld a constant state of psychological warfare, in which one person's vanity battled another's for supremacy.

94

Oscar Wilde quipped that

To love oneself is the beginning of a lifelong romance.

But La Rochefoucauld's *amour-propre* is a far darker, more complex and sinister emotion. No one is immune, and even our most laudable virtues are infected by the taint of this vice. Modesty, for example, is not true humility but a clever ruse to elicit yet more accolades:

To refuse to accept praise is to want to be praised twice over.

A compliment given to another is just a down payment on the compliment expected in return:

We seldom praise except to get praise back.

Loyalty and friendship are based not on mutual regard but on a cold calculation of the other person's potential usefulness:

We find few guilty of ingratitude while we are still in a position to help them.

The *Maxims* are filled with these kinds of dark reflections on human nature, which have surprising parallels in contemporary ideas of evolutionary psychology. According to Darwinian theory, our genes are selfish, interested solely in their own survival and propagation. The entire point of evolution, in fact, is to maximize the genetic and biological

95

advantages that increase an organism's chances of surviving and reproducing. 'Natural selection will never produce in a being any structure more injurious than beneficial to that being, for natural selection acts solely by and for the good of each,' Charles Darwin explained.

Evolutionary psychology suggests that our emotions, like our bodies, also act solely 'by and for the good of each'. Feelings such as kindness, altruism and generosity are actually subtle evolutionary strategies to further the petty interests of our genes. We tend to love our offspring and family members most intensely, for example, because they too bear copies of our genes. In genetic terms, their success is our success. 'The dispersed copies of a gene call to one another by endowing bodies with emotions. Love, compassion, and empathy are invisible fibers that connect genes in different bodies . . . People helping relatives equals genes helping themselves,' writes evolutionary psychologist Steven Pinker.

Taken out of the realm of biology and applied to the realm of morality, this is a fair description of *amour-propre*. Pick any supposed virtue and La Rochefoucauld is ready with the darker, more selfish explanation for its appeal. Why do we rush to the aid of family and friends in need? Not because of genuine concern but because:

Pity is often feeling our own sufferings in those of others, a shrewd precaution against misfortunes that may befall us. We give help to others so that they have to do the same for us on similar occasions, and these kindnesses we do them are, to put it plainly, gifts we bestow on ourselves in advance.

96

Why do we praise thrift and disdain ostentation? Not because frugality is inherently good but because:

Moderation in times of good fortune is merely dread of the humiliating aftermath of excess, or fear of losing what one has.

Why do we refrain from stealing our neighbour's property, even though we may ardently covet it? Not because we're law-abiding citizens but because:

Justice is no more than lively fear that our belongings will be taken away from us. This is at the root of men's consideration and respect for all the interests of others, and their scrupulous care never to do them wrong.

When La Rochefoucauld published his *Maxims* in 1665, the public was scandalized by their savage cynicism. His spare, desiccated aphorisms are definitely not for the faint-hearted. He is merciless in his dissection of the human soul, coldly clinical in his diagnosis. Reading La Rochefoucauld is like poring over some gruesomely exact anatomy book: we're fascinated even as we flinch. These are awful truths, but truths nonetheless:

The reason for so much outcry against maxims that lay bare the human heart is that people are afraid of having their own laid bare.

97

## Luc de Clapiers, Marquis de Vauvenargues (1715–1747)
### The Necessity of Virtue

Vauvenargues agreed with La Rochefoucauld about the power of aphorisms to lay bare the human heart. In fact, one of his characteristically direct and unadorned sayings ('Clearness is the ornament of deep thought,' he wrote) echoes that of the disillusioned duke:

The maxims of men reveal their hearts.

But that's about the only thing on which these two aphorists agreed. La Rochefoucauld saw deceit, betrayal and crass opportunism in the heart laid bare; Vauvenargues saw heroism, virtue and glory there. The two men are opposites in many ways: Vauvenargues was shy, unworldly and introspective; La Rochefoucauld was smooth, urbane and rakish. Yet their lives had many parallels: both had lacklustre military careers; both were vexed by their failure to win favour at court; and both ultimately concluded that society was a vicious, demeaning charade. The one big difference was that Vauvenargues didn't live long enough to benefit from the wisdom of old age.

Born in Aix-en-Provence in southern France, the eldest son of a family of minor nobility, Vauvenargues was a sickly child who had defective eyesight. His poor vision and even poorer general health often kept him home from school, so he never received the grounding in the classics that most of his contemporaries enjoyed. But that suited the young Vauvenargues just fine. He disdained literature and learning anyway. He wanted a life of action and was convinced that greatness and glory were his destiny. So at about the age of seventeen, he joined the army.

Vauvenargues would have subscribed wholeheartedly to William Blake's dictum:

Energy is eternal delight.

But sadly, he had little of either. He dreamed of valour on the battlefield, but his health held him back and he lacked the necessary connections to secure advancement up the ranks.

In 1741, during the War of the Austrian Succession, Vauvenargues' regiment marched all the way to Prague in the dead of winter and occupied the city. It was a great victory, at least until the French came under siege from Austrian forces and started running out of food, water and ammunition. Facing a slow, freezing defeat in Prague, the French broke out and made a desperate dash south through one of the fiercest cold spells on record. During the long, ignominious march Vauvenargues' legs became frostbitten, disabling him for the rest of his life, and he contracted the pulmonary disease that killed him four years later.

After Prague, Vauvenargues was a disappointed man. He longed for action and glory, but fate and his health conspired against them, no doubt prompting one of his more rueful musings:

The greatest evil that fortune can bring to men is to endow them with feeble resources and yet to make them ambitious.

99

But Vauvenargues did not despair. If anything, he became even more determined to fulfil his destiny by other means. Politics seemed the obvious choice, and he focused his ambitions on the Foreign Ministry.

Vauvenargues had absolutely no qualifications for a job, so he highlighted his strength of character where his résumé was deficient. He wrote astonishingly pushy letters to ministry officials demanding a post in the diplomatic corps. When they politely declined, he penned a plea for help to Voltaire, who was then at the peak of his fame. The great man must have spotted promise in Vauvenargues' prose, and a shared passion for aphorisms, because the two struck up an epistolary friendship and Voltaire encouraged the young soldier to come to Paris to take up literature.

With no family fortune to fall back on, Vauvenargues desperately needed a source of income, and it was clear that neither the military nor the diplomatic corps was going to provide it. Yet he still hadn't lost his ambition. He hated the fatuity of his times and was determined not to be beaten into complacency. So he promptly forgot his previous disdain for the life of letters and in 1746 published a little book containing some essays and a selection of his maxims.

Vauvenargues' debut attracted scant attention, and he could not but have reflected on the disparity between his youthful dreams of adventure and glory and the reality of his present life scribbling away in obscurity in a shabby Parisian garret. Yet he wouldn't give up; he couldn't follow any other course:

Necessity saves us the trouble of choosing.

For Vauvenargues, necessity was the mother of ambition. Despite repeated setbacks, and the by now clear evidence of his failing health, he never lost faith in himself. He felt he had no other option: he was meant for greatness, whether in the arts, diplomacy or war. He never scaled back his aspirations, either. He always thought big – he planned but never completed the modestly entitled tome, *Introduction to the Knowledge of the Human Mind* – and regarded each rebuff as an opportunity to think even bigger:

He who knows how to suffer everything can dare everything.

Vauvenargues accepted that this all-consuming ambition was an aspect of La Rochefoucauld's *amour-propre*, but he argued that it was a virtue not a vice. His brand of enlightened self-love was the source of both ambition and achievement, a spur to excellence rather than an appeal to vanity or conceit. He believed that self-love was a positive and productive force: it drives us to test our limits, impels us to do our best, and compels us not to settle for anything less:

Consciousness of our strength increases it.

To Vauvenargues, the imperatives of *amour-propre* meant there could be no compromise or retreat. His family urged him to come back to Aix, where they could support him financially and hopefully nurse him back to health. But he stayed in Paris, his condition becoming progressively worse, preferring to keep his dream alive rather than return to what he felt was the pettiness and provincialism of his home town. His family could only have thought this was madness; he surely thought he had no other choice:

Men of parts seldom think of questioning anything else but what other people hold beyond question.

Vauvenargues died in Paris at the age of thirty-two. His short life was filled with disappointments and defeats, yet he never lost his virtuous ambition, or his belief in himself. Given all that he was up against, that in itself is an extraordinary achievement. He is the prototype of the struggling, impecunious artist, the brilliant but untutored amateur, the self-made man who never quite made it. His aphorisms challenge us to have the strength of our convictions, pushing us up the path of most persistence lest we fall into a rut so deep we forget we ever dreamed of glory at all:

Most men grow old in a little groove of notions which they have not originated: perhaps there are fewer crooked minds than barren ones.

## Sébastien-Roch-Nicolas Chamfort (1740–94)
## A Thousand Clashing Petty Interests

Chamfort's life story could have come straight from the pages of a Charles Dickens novel. He was born in Clermont-Ferrand in central France, to a mother descended from minor nobility and a father who was not her husband. History's best guess is that Chamfort's father was a canon at Clermont Cathedral. At the time, it was common for men to have illegitimate children but for women it was socially unacceptable. So Chamfort's mother desperately sought a way to dispose of her boy.

As fate would have it, the infant son of a local grocer passed away on the same day that Chamfort was born. Chamfort's mother delicately suggested a quiet adoption. The grocer agreed. So the young Chamfort was adopted and given the dead child's name: Sébastien-Roch-Nicolas. It was only when the changeling was eight years old that his biological mother revealed to him his true lineage.

The strange tale of Chamfort's youth branded him for life. As an adult, he was both proud of his identity – he insisted on adopting the name of his mother's husband, Chamfort – but bitter at being deprived of the wealth and privilege he felt belonged to him. He developed a kind of split personality as a result: he both despised and admired the aristocracy; he was a leading republican during the Revolution yet actively sought favour and patrons at court; he professed disdain for riches and renown but was extremely adept in seeking them out.

Apart from the accident of his birth, Chamfort had much to recommend him. He was handsome, charming, witty and cunning, everything Vauvenargues was not. By the time he was twenty, he had established himself as a brilliant student, promising playwright and celebrated lover. He seemed destined for the fame and fortune denied him at birth. From his station as the boy genius of Paris, Chamfort unleashed his aphoristic assault on the French Establishment.

Chamfort was an eighteenth-century Andy Warhol,

someone who managed to ridicule and critique high society from a prominent position within it. Like Warhol, he was fascinated by fame, what it meant and how to get it. Indeed, many of Chamfort's maxims have a distinctly contemporary resonance. In Chamfort's time, sycophancy and subterfuge were how you made your name:

Courtiers are poor men who have become rich by begging.

In our own day, people get their fifteen minutes by baring all on 'reality' television shows, but to Chamfort the motivation is the same:

In a country where everyone is trying to be noticed, it is better to be bankrupt than to be nothing.

Chamfort was deeply ambivalent about this craving for fame. He routinely derided it:

Celebrity: the advantage of being known by those who do not know you.

But he was also a scheming social climber par excellence and delivered these withering denouncements from the comfort of the most prestigious salons in Paris. Chamfort was very much aware, though completely untroubled, by the contradictions. He had already concluded that society was all artifice, calculation and contrivance. So he felt no compunction about slapping down with one hand what he rapaciously grasped with the other. And, besides, hypocrisy was among the least reprehensible traits the well-intentioned courtier might come across:

A man must swallow a toad every morning if he wishes to be sure of finding nothing still more disgusting before the day is over.

In his mid-twenties, Chamfort's luck began to change. His first play was widely praised, but his subsequent efforts bombed and he struggled to recoup his reputation as an up-and-comer. He also contracted a debilitating illness, possibly venereal, that ruined his looks and left him weak and listless. His popularity with women faded. By the age of twenty-five, Chamfort had gone from being the playboy of the Parisian literati to a near-invalid whose best work was already behind him.

Chamfort's reaction was typical of the pattern he followed throughout his life: whenever he met with failure or rejection, he affected to despise whatever had been denied him. So he retreated from the salons, from Paris and from society at large to live with his lover, Marthe Buffon, who tragically died just six months into their relationship.

With Buffon's death, Chamfort was once again robbed of something he felt rightly belonged to him: true love. Grief further darkened his already grim view of fate. His aphorisms become more gloomy and acerbic, his verdict on human nature more severe. He concluded that even our most exalted emotions are polluted by *amour-propre* and he felt cruelly deluded by his youthful ambitions:

Society, which is called the world, is nothing but the contention of a thousand clashing petty interests, an eternal conflict of all the vanities that cross each other, strike against each other, are wounded and humiliated by each other in turn, and expiate on the morrow, in the bitterness of defeat, the triumph of the day before. To live alone, to avoid the bruises of wretched scrapes in which one attracts all eyes one minute only to be trampled on the next, is to be what they call nothing, to have no existence. Poor humanity!

With Buffon gone, his health shattered and his career on the rocks, Chamfort just didn't see the point any more. Yet when the Revolution came, Chamfort was one of its shrewdest spokesmen and most enthusiastic supporters. He was among the first to enter the Bastille after it was stormed. His political maxims are just as caustic as his moral reflections, and many of his sayings became revolutionary slogans and may occasionally still be overheard at suitably grand cocktail parties:

Society is made up of two great classes: those who have more dinners than appetite, and those who have more appetite than dinners.

But Chamfort was also wary, fearing the Revolution could go wrong. For all his professed aversion to the aristocracy, he mistrusted the mob even more. He knew that by giving power to the people the revolutionaries might well just end up supplanting one form of dictatorship with another.

Chamfort's misgivings proved well founded. Chaos and terror soon followed liberation, and the perceived enemies of the Revolution were rounded up and sent either to jail or to the guillotine. Outspoken as ever, Chamfort was critical of the new regime's excesses and, ironically, his noble name came back to haunt him. He was accused of being an aristocrat, arrested for sedition and detained in one of Paris's foulest prisons. He was released after two days, but his stay in the fetid, rat-infested cell traumatized him. He vowed never to allow himself to be sent back.

A few weeks later, Chamfort was in the middle of dinner with friends when the gendarmes arrived to take him in for questioning. He calmly finished his soup and coffee before withdrawing to his dressing room, where he took out a pistol concealed there for just such an occasion. This is a friend's account of what happened next:

He shut himself in, loaded a pistol, intending to fire at his forehead, smashed the upper part of his nose and burst his right eye. Surprised to find himself alive, and determined to die, he seized a razor and tried to cut his throat, renewing the attempt several times and cutting all the flesh to tatters . . . He dealt himself several blows, trying to reach the heart, and in a final effort, on the verge of fainting, he tried to cut both his wrists and open all his veins. At last overcome with pain, he cried out and fell into a chair, where he stayed, almost dead. The blood flowed under the door in streams.

Chamfort inflicted a total of twenty-two separate wounds on himself, none of which was immediately fatal. He lingered on for a few months, but it was clearly only a matter of time. 'What can you expect?' he said. 'That's what it is to be clumsy with one's hands. One never manages to do anything successfully, even killing oneself.'

Chamfort never published his aphorisms during his lifetime. His practice was to jot his thoughts down on little scraps of paper and then deposit them haphazardly in boxes. After his death, dozens of these boxes were found scattered around his flat. But many of them later disappeared and were presumed stolen. So Chamfort's maxims, collected in *Products of the Perfected Civilization*, are only a small part of what he actually wrote.

The sayings that survived are still incredibly pungent. Reading them is like sniffing camphor: one whiff brings you back to reality with a jolt. It's difficult to entertain any illusions about yourself or others under the influence of Chamfort.

For all his conflicts and contradictions, Chamfort's last act was consistent with his lifelong habit of rejecting what others were about to take away from him. In the end, his suicide prevented the regime from taking away his liberty. Perhaps that was his final victory:

He who leaves the game wins it.

## Joseph Joubert (1754–1824)
### An Accursed Ambition

Joubert was the least worldly of all the great French aphorists. He abhorred the military, shunned politics and was more comfortable in his own study than in the Parisian salons. He lived through the Revolution, but played no part in it. He devoted himself almost exclusively to literature and contemplation, far removed from the daily grind of getting and spending. His model was Montaigne, whom he regarded as a kindred spirit. Yet Joubert was unlike Montaigne in one very important respect: Montaigne sustained his *Essays* for over 1,200 pages; Joubert never managed to write a book.

In fact, except for a handful of reports compiled in 1809 as inspector general of the University of France (one of his rare periods of actual employment), Joubert never completed any piece of writing at all. Even his correspondence, which is voluminous, never seems quite finished. He invariably appended postscripts to his letters, sometimes several. He was endlessly revising and refining his ideas, and some crucial afterthought always seemed to occur to him just as he was about to seal the envelope.

'I love blank paper more than ever,' Joubert wrote to a friend, explaining a long gap between letters, 'and I no longer wish to give myself the trouble of expressing carefully any thoughts but those worthy of being written upon silk or upon bronze.' This may sound like a hopelessly precious excuse for being a poor correspondent, but Joubert was a perfectionist. He couldn't abide imprecision of thought or expression in himself or others. If he read an inelegant or clumsy passage in an otherwise good book, he ripped the offending page out. His goal was to distil the essence of a thought into its purest, most succinct and most concentrated form:

I polish not my phrase, but my idea. I linger till the drop of light I need forms and falls from my pen.

If that distillate didn't come, Joubert preferred to leave the page blank:

If there is a man tormented by the accursed ambition to put a whole book in a page, a whole page in a sentence, and that sentence in one word, I am he.

What Joubert did manage to get down on paper are his beguiling *pensées*, the thoughts and reflections he recorded in his notebooks between 1774 and 1824. For a man obsessed with order, Joubert left his manuscripts in a total mess. The *pensées* were contained in around two hundred notebooks, sixty bundles of papers and innumerable letters left scattered in various boxes and drawers when he died. Many of these 'scraps of paper', as he called them, bear Joubert's luminous insights on the art and craft of the aphorism itself. Joubert was fascinated by the maxim, and his notebooks reveal him as an accomplished theorist as well as practitioner of the form:

These thoughts form not only the foundation of my work, but of my life.

That life was mostly uneventful. Joubert was born in 1754 in the little town of Martignac in the Dordogne, just up the road from the famous prehistoric cave paintings of Lascaux. At fourteen, he went to Toulouse to study law, but ended up joining the religious order of the Doctrinaires instead. Neither the law nor the priesthood attracted him, though, so in 1778 he went to Paris, where he was befriended by Diderot and some of the other encyclopedists, who urged him to take up essay-writing.

Joubert was a prim, fastidious figure and – like a surprising number of great aphorists, both ancient and modern – a hypochondriac. He would spend days in bed complaining of nebulous ailments and strange languors, often inflicting eccentric diets on himself: one day he would drink only milk, the next eat only meat. He married Adélaïde Victoire Moreau in 1793 and, disgusted by the tyranny of the revolutionists, retired to his wife's estate in Villeneuve-le-Roi. Except for his brief stint as inspector general of the University of France, Joubert remained there for the rest of his life.

Joubert was a thinker rather than a doer, a man of independent means and abundant leisure who never had a job and never wanted one. His aphorisms retain a kind of remote grandeur, a sense of aloofness from the mundane business of living. He has none of the corrosive wit that sizzles in the sayings of Chamfort, none of the grit of Montaigne. He has absolutely nothing to say about the hypocrisy of social relationships, the illusion of virtue or the delusions of self-love. Joubert's major theme is his 'accursed ambition' to squeeze an entire book into a single, perfect word. This makes him the great apostle of the aphorism:

Maxims are to the intelligence what laws are to action: they do not illuminate, but they guide, they control, they rescue blindly. They are the clue in the labyrinth, the ship's compass in the night.

Joubert's *pensées* can be labyrinthine themselves. There are plenty of clues to his meaning, but they are often difficult to follow. What he wrote of poets is true of aphorists as well:

The poet must not cross an interval with a step when he can cross it with a leap.

Deft imaginative leaps give aphorisms their ability to startle and delight, but readers need to be pretty nimble to keep up. The difficulty arises because the aphorist never pauses to describe what he's doing. He just jumps. Whether we land on our feet is entirely down to us.

This is especially true of Joubert, whose goal was to produce from the great mass of verbiage in the world a few simple, shining sentences. To find these phrases, both reader and writer traverse the same tangled paths, both require the same type of mental agility, and both experience the same kind of amazement when they arrive at the aphorism's heart. So for Joubert, reading an aphorism was practically identical to writing one:

To penetrate a thought and to produce a thought are almost the same action.

Joubert achieved the element of surprise through rigour and precision, practice and perfectionism. He recognized that an aphorism is only as great as the idea behind it, and he was willing to wait until both his idea and its expression were ripe. He was out to catch a thought in mid-flight, to capture an idea while it still burned bright, and to do that required an almost infinite patience:

What I should wish is for thoughts to follow each other, in a book, like stars in the heavens in order, harmoniously, yet at leisurely intervals, without jostling, without confusion, yet not without proper sequence, harmony and arrangement. I should wish them lastly to wheel about, without holding together, so as to be able to subsist independently, like unthreaded pearls.

Joubert's aphorisms are indeed like stars: their light is sometimes faint and often takes a while to reach us, but in constellation they have a majestic elegance. Though his biography may seem thin, Joubert lived a passionate and adventurous life of the mind. His belief in the reality of ideas – and the brilliance of their expression – explains why his own aphorisms, and those of the other great French and Spanish moralists, still strike us with maximum impact:

A thought is a thing as real as a cannon ball.

# 4 Good and evil are the prejudices of God:

## Heretics, Dissenters and Sceptics

On 27 July 1656, Baruch de Spinoza, the twenty-three-year-old son of a prominent Amsterdam merchant, was excommunicated from the city's Portuguese-Jewish community. The edict announcing his expulsion was the harshest ever pronounced by Amsterdam's Jewish leaders and, unlike similar decrees regularly handed out as punishment for a variety of religious or social misdeeds, it didn't offer Spinoza the chance to repent and rejoin the congregation. He was henceforth to be regarded as a permanent outcast:

The Lords of [Spinoza's synagogue in Amsterdam], having long known of the evil opinions and acts of Baruch de Spinoza [and] daily receiving more and more serious information about the abominable heresies which he practised and taught and about his monstrous deeds . . . excommunicate, expel, curse and damn Baruch de Spinoza . . . Cursed be he by day and cursed be he by night; cursed be he when he lies down and cursed be he when he rises up. Cursed be he when he goes out and cursed be he when he comes in.

As if that wasn't enough, no one – including members of Spinoza's own family – was permitted to communicate with him in any way, conduct any type of business with him, read anything he had written, or even come within 'four cubits' of his person. What had this frail, reclusive young man done to incur the wrath of Amsterdam's Portuguese-Jewish elders?

Though the order doesn't list Spinoza's 'abominable heresies' by name, and at the time of his excommunication he hadn't yet published anything, Spinoza was already well known as one of the freest thinkers in a famously freethinking city. But even in Amsterdam tolerance had its limits. Spinoza's reputation as a popularizer of Descartes' rationalistic thought made him suspect; rumours of his own radical thinking fuelled his vilification.

Spinoza denied that the human soul was immortal; dismissed heaven and hell as silly superstitions; argued that sacred scripture was not divinely revealed but compiled, edited and manipulated by human beings; decried organized religions as purveyors of fear, ignorance and prejudice; and rejected the idea of a personalized, loving God in favour of one that was identical with nature and indifferent to human fate. So the lords of the synagogue had plenty of monstrous ideas to choose from.

Spinoza didn't seem to take much notice of his excommunication, though. He was quite content to keep to himself and had probably already jettisoned the business obligations he inherited when his father died about ten years earlier. So his expulsion had only a minimal impact on his day-to-day life. He took up lens-grinding to earn a living, was careful about what he published and with whom he shared his thoughts, and dedicated himself to building on Descartes' ideas about the supremacy of human reason.

In *Principles of Cartesian Philosophy*, a kind of 'Descartes for Dummies' published in 1663, Spinoza distilled the French philosopher's system into an elegant set of axioms and definitions. Spinoza took Descartes' mathematical approach to metaphysics seriously. Starting from a handful of self-evident propositions – such as 'I think, therefore I am' – he constructed tautly argued proofs of Cartesian philosophy by stacking up interlocking axioms like philosophical Lego bricks. One axiom provided the foundation on which the next one was built.

Spinoza called this style of philosophical argument the 'geometric method' because he tried to present his ideas with an exactitude and irrefutability that approached mathematics. 'I shall consider human actions and desires in exactly the same manner, as though I were concerned with lines, planes and solids,' he wrote. In *The Ethics*, a treatise on the nature of God, the human mind and the emotions, he used the geometric method to answer the question that occupied him most: 'whether, in fact, there might be anything of which the discovery and attainment would enable me to enjoy continuous, supreme and unending happiness'.

In *The Ethics*, Spinoza solves this oldest and most vexing of problems through the axiom, a kind of proto-aphorism that takes the second law of aphorisms – it must be definitive – to extremes. An axiom is so absolutely, positively true that it's taken as a given. Spinoza meticulously lists a lexicon of human emotions – ranging from pleasure, pain and envy to contempt, merriment and melancholy – and for each one offers his own axiomatic explanation. His definition of love, for example, may not be very romantic but it is clinically accurate:

Love is nothing else but pleasure accompanied by the idea of an external cause.

In this way, Spinoza establishes a palette of primary emotions, the psychological equivalents of Descartes' self-evident propositions. He then goes on to show how each emotion has its obverse – hate, for example, is just pain accompanied by the idea of an external cause – and how basic instincts such as these give rise to all other emotions and, ultimately, to all forms of human behaviour. His dissection of hope and fear is a marvel of precision:

Hope is nothing else but an inconstant pleasure, arising from the image of something future or past, whereof we do not yet know the issue. Fear, on the other hand, is an inconstant pain also arising from the image of something concerning which we are in doubt. If the element of doubt be removed from these emotions, hope becomes confidence and fear becomes despair.

Spinoza is the spiritual and literary forefather of the great philosopher-aphorists of the eighteenth, nineteenth and twentieth centuries. Like him, they were all iconoclasts; some proclaiming the death of God, others praising the birth of their own new creeds. Like him, they all rejected received wisdom – from the Church, the state or the community – and embraced individual enlightenment as the sole gauge of truth. And like him, they all attempted to solve the great equations of the spirit with their own variations on the geometric method. Though their philosophies differ, these heretics, dissenters and sceptics would all agree with Spinoza's answer to the question he posed in *The Ethics*:

Happiness or unhappiness is made wholly to depend on the quality of the object which we love.

## Georg Christoph Lichtenberg (1742–99)
### The Enlightenment's Aphorist

Lichtenberg was an archetypal Enlightenment scholar. A scientist by training and profession, he was an accomplished physicist, mathematician and astronomer, and one of the first people in history to conduct actual experiments. He was also something of an amateur psychologist. More than a century before Freud, he scrupulously recorded his dreams and speculated about how dream analysis could reveal our inner lives. He authored numerous scientific papers, edited the *Göttingen Pocket Almanac* for more than twenty years, and produced an early map of the moon – there's even a crater named after him. But Lichtenberg was an aphorist at heart, and much preferred the study of human beings to the scrutiny of heavenly bodies:

The most entertaining surface on earth is the human face.

Born in Oberramstadt, near Darmstadt, Germany, the youngest of seventeen children, Lichtenberg was a weak and sickly child, suffering from a malformation of the spine that later made him a hunchback. He was plagued by poor health throughout his life and, like Joseph Joubert, became an inveterate hypochondriac, creating a host of imaginary maladies to accompany his real illnesses.

Lichtenberg's father, who died when Georg was just nine, was a prominent Lutheran minister, part of a reformist movement called Pietism that emphasized the Bible and counselled its adherents to live a life of simple Christian virtue. But Lichtenberg lost his faith as a teenager. He was an empiricist, even in matters of the soul, and all his scientific and literary work – especially his aphorisms – sings the praises of enlightened scepticism:

Doubt everything at least once, even the proposition that twice two is four.

Lichtenberg became a lecturer at the University of Göttingen and quickly established a reputation as a scientist and philosopher. (His aphorisms weren't discovered until after his death.) He was friends with Goethe (also a prolific, if ponderous, aphorist) and corresponded with Kant, but was best known as an eager and entertaining popularizer of the young science of electricity. He erected Göttingen's first lightning rod and gave crowd-pleasing talks at his home which featured spectacular displays of electrical special effects.

He also accidentally discovered Lichtenberg figures, also known as electron trees, the branch- or star-like patterns created in dust and other powders when disturbed by a burst of electricity. It's only fitting that Lichtenberg gave his name to these vivid shapes since his aphorisms have all the crackle and fizz of lightning bolts – and provide the same kind of stark, sudden clarity:

The fly that does not want to be swatted is safest if it sits on the fly-swat.

Lichtenberg illuminates his universe not with big bangs but through quick flashes. But his inspiration came slowly. He practised what he called the 'waste-book method' of composition. With all the careful attention of a researcher nurturing an important mould in a Petri dish, Lichtenberg observed himself and those around him, then recorded this raw data in the notebooks he kept from 1765 until his death in 1799.

Lichtenberg's notebooks are crammed with the meticulously recorded minutiae of his daily experience: memoranda to himself, remarks on books to be read or purchased, quotes from scientific papers and magazines, comments on the great philosophical debates of the time, and his own random ideas and observations. He took this 'waste' of facts and notions and refined it into witty, flippant aphorisms.

'Merchants have a waste-book . . . in which they enter from day to day everything they have bought and sold, all mixed up together in disorder,' Lichtenberg wrote.

From this it is transferred to the journal, in which everything is arranged more systematically; and finally it arrives in the ledger . . . This deserves to be imitated by the scholar. First a book in which I inscribe everything just as I see it or as my thoughts prompt me, then this can be transferred to another where the materials are more ordered and segregated, and the ledger can then contain a connected construction and the elucidation of the subject that flows from it expressed in an orderly fashion.

But as a devout sceptic, Lichtenberg knew that his tidy aphorisms offered just a glimpse of the truth and not the whole picture:

Do not judge God's world from your own. Trim your hedge as you wish and plant your flowers in the patterns you can understand, but do not judge the garden of nature from your little window-box.

Lichtenberg mined his waste-books for some of the eighteenth century's brightest aphoristic treasures. With his sharp eye for spotting poignant quotidian imagery and even sharper mind for exposing sloppy, unscientific thinking, he was a strange mix of poet, scientist, philosopher and comedian. His aphorisms charm with their sense of ebullience and humour, but they also challenge us to accept the uncomfortable fact that doubt is the highest form of knowledge. Lichtenberg is one of those rare writers whose words produce as much light as heat:

It is impossible to carry the torch of truth through a crowd without singeing someone's beard.

## Arthur Schopenhauer (1788–1860)
### The Buddha of Frankfurt

The preface to the first edition of *The World as Will and Representation*, Schopenhauer's magnum opus, published in 1819, is not exactly what you'd expect from one of the nineteenth century's great aphorists. The book, Schopenhauer wrote, is intended to convey 'a single thought. Yet in spite of all my efforts, I have not been able to find a shorter way of imparting that thought than the whole of this book'. Sadly for readers in search of a quick philosophical fix, the whole of this book totalled almost 1,100 pages by 1844 when the second and final edition came out.

Fortunately, Schopenhauer grew more concise with age, though, like Balthasar Gracían (whose work he loved, translating it into German in the 1820s), he remained a practitioner of the long-form aphorism throughout his life. His ruminations range from a few sentences to a few paragraphs in length, but always contain a discrete aphoristic core, one or two sentences that condense and complete his thought. In fact, it was his aphorisms – published in 1851 as part of the essays and reflections contained in his second and last book, *Parerga and Paralipomena* – which first won Schopenhauer popular acclaim.

During the previous thirty-two years, he and his philosophy had been virtually ignored. His fellow thinkers dismissed him as a crank and curmudgeon, while what he considered his masterpiece – he once described *The World as Will and Representation* as 'the real solution of the enigma of the world . . . There are even some paragraphs which may be considered to be dictated by the Holy Ghost' – went almost completely unread. It was a humiliating ordeal for a man of Schopenhauer's cantankerous intellect and colossal arrogance, and may have provided the emotional backdrop to one of his pithier, more Spinozan observations:

Hope is the confusion of the desire for a thing with its probability.

As improbable as it seemed at the time, Schopenhauer was eventually recognized for his philosophical genius. In the 1820s, during an ill-fated career as a university lecturer, he couldn't attract a single student to his classes; by the 1850s, people would crowd into the Englischer Hof, Schopenhauer's favourite Frankfurt restaurant, just to watch the eccentric thinker eat lunch.

It wasn't difficult to catch Schopenhauer satisfying his prodigious appetite; he regularly dined at the Englischer Hof as part of a daily routine that rarely varied during the twenty-seven years he lived in Frankfurt. Schopenhauer rose every day at 7 a.m., took a bath, drank a cup of coffee and wrote until noon. Then he played the flute for an hour and headed to the Englischer Hof for lunch. After his meal, he read until four and then went for a brisk two-hour constitutional, accompanied by his poodle. At 6 p.m. he stopped by the library to read the London *Times* and in the evening had dinner at a restaurant, attended the theatre or a concert, and was in bed by 10 p.m.

This life of literature and leisure was made possible by Schopenhauer's father, a wealthy merchant who committed suicide by throwing himself out of the window of one of his

Hamburg warehouses. As a result, when Schopenhauer turned twenty-one, he inherited a small fortune that allowed him to focus on philosophy without having to worry about earning a living. He could now afford to declare that 'Life is an unpleasant business; I have resolved to spend it reflecting upon it'.

The result of these reflections is neatly summed up in the title of Schopenhauer's first book. The world, Schopenhauer thought, is double. The realm of material objects is a creation, or representation, of the mind that apprehends it. The external world therefore depends on a seeing subject for its existence. 'To be is to be perceived,' as Bishop Berkeley put it. The will, however, exists independently. It is the primary force that drives all living things and natural processes. It is the blind striving behind our struggle to survive, the most basic of our basest instincts.

The will – selfish, egotistical and tenacious – is also what makes life such an unpleasant business. Conflict and suffering are the only possible results in a world where billions of wills collide. Happiness, then, is not a thing in itself but merely the absence of pain; its pursuit consists in extinguishing the will, thus escaping the wretched game:

The good things we possess, or are certain of getting, are not felt to be such; because all pleasure is in fact of a negative nature and effects the relief of pain, while pain or evil is what is really positive; it is the object of immediate sensation.

That, in short, is the basis of Schopenhauer's thought. It's also a pretty fair approximation of Buddha's original teaching that suffering exists and the cause of suffering is clinging – to our thoughts, our desires, our wills. Schopenhauer had formulated his own ideas before he began his intensive reading of Buddhist philosophy, but he recognized that the conclusions of both systems derived from the same insights. 'In my seventeenth year, without any learned school education, I was gripped by the misery of life as Buddha was in his youth when he saw sickness, old age, pain and death,' Schopenhauer wrote in 1832.

But Buddha and Schopenhauer diverged on one crucial point. Whereas Schopenhauer believed the will was the permanent element in everything, Buddha taught that the will – or the self, in Buddhist terminology – was just as illusory as all other mental constructs. Schopenhauer's strategies for overcoming the will are different, too. Though in *The World as Will and Representation* he recommends a practice of focused attention that could have come straight from a Buddhist meditation manual, Schopenhauer also believed we could transcend the will through artistic creation and contemplation. We can lose ourselves, and drown our wills, by absorption in making and appreciating works of art, a process whereby the perceiver and perceived become one.

Apart from these higher moments of aesthetic consciousness, Schopenhauer took a pretty dim view of things. People are vain and untrustworthy, he warned, and anguish and disappointment are pretty much all we can expect:

Virtue is a stranger in this world; and boundless egoism, cunning and malice are always the order of the day. It is wrong to deceive the young on this point, for it will only make them feel later on that their teachers were the first to deceive them.

Despite his virulent pessimism, Schopenhauer was determined to extract the maximum amount of happiness from life. The surest way to do that, he thought, was to wage war against the will, to ruthlessly extirpate all its tendrils and twinings. But slaying the will is a task for saints and philosophers. For the rest of us, Schopenhauer advised a Stoic approach: find out how things work, and then accept it.

There are three sources of pleasure and self-esteem, Schopenhauer reasoned: that which comes from possessions, or what a person has; that which comes from reputation, or what a person represents to others; and that which comes from personality, or what a person is. The first two are the most fickle and least reliable since they are wholly out of our control. Possessions can be destroyed or stolen, and reputation can be lost through no fault of our own, so it's risky to base happiness on those. Our personalities, however, are ours alone. We are what we will, and everyone's will is different. The trick is to yield to what our wills demand from us, to be in harmony with ourselves by desiring to become who we already are:

It is a harmony which produces an agreeable and rational character; and for the simple reason that everything which makes the man and gives him his mental and physical qualities is nothing but the manifestation of his will; is, in fact, what he wills. Therefore it is the greatest of all inconsistencies to wish to be other than we are.

126

Not wishing to be other than we are sounds simple enough, but for Schopenhauer it was a torturous existential crisis. First, you must make a merciless personal inventory cataloguing all your vices and virtues, your fine points and foibles. Then you must smother all those expressions of your will that threaten to drive you off in the wrong direction.

It's sensible advice to vie against the lesser angels of our nature. Once you've identified undesirable traits, why not snuff them out? The regular pruning of unproductive or withered shoots can lead to greater personal growth. But Schopenhauer makes clear that we should expect no great victory from this brutal, wilful struggle. Life remains mostly misery, our aspirations mostly thwarted, the reward for our efforts mostly derisory – so you'd better get used to it:

A good supply of resignation is of the first importance in providing for the journey of life. It is a supply which we shall have to extract from disappointed hopes; and the sooner we do it, the better for the rest of the journey.

## Friedrich Nietzsche (1844–1900)
### Shouting from the Mountain tops

One of Schopenhauer's most enthusiastic fellow travellers on the will's grim journey was Friedrich Nietzsche. In 1865, as a twenty-one-year-old student of classical philology, Nietzsche came across a copy of *The World as Will and Representation* in a second-hand bookshop in Leipzig and it immediately changed his life. He read and re-read the book in a fever of excitement over the next two weeks, and later incorporated adaptations of Schopenhauer's ideas about the will and redemption through art into his own philosophy. He embraced Schopenhauer's assertion that there is no God, and no meaning inherent in the universe except what we give to it:

Truths are illusions of which one has forgotten that they *are* illusions.

Like Schopenhauer, Nietzsche led an outwardly uneventful life. The son of a pious Lutheran minister, he was a devout and obedient child who could recite biblical verses from memory and often sang church hymns to himself. Fellow students called him 'the little pastor', an ironic nickname for someone who later became famous for proclaiming the death of God.

Nietzsche was always something of a prodigy, though. He became a professor of classical philology at the age of twenty-four and Richard Wagner was a great admirer of his first book, *The Birth of Tragedy*. The unknown young philosopher and the world's most famous composer were close friends for a while, until Nietzsche (an amateur pianist and composer himself) came to despise Wagner's music and the two had an acrimonious falling out.

Nietzsche's academic career was cut short by ill health. He was plagued by migraines, dysentery and diphtheria, the latter infection picked up in 1870 while serving as a medical orderly during the Franco-Prussian War. He probably also contracted syphilis from a prostitute some time in the late 1870s, a condition that gradually eroded his nervous system and eventually led to his insanity. In 1879 he resigned his teaching post, received a small annual stipend and, until madness struck him down ten years later, roamed around northern Italy and the Swiss Alps in search of a place that would restore his health and allow him the time and solitude in which to write.

Nietzsche, like Schopenhauer, loved hiking in the mountains, and in the summer of 1881 he had an epiphany in the Alps near the Swiss town of Sils-Maria: a vision of a prophet coming down from the mountains to announce the death of God and tell the human race that it was time to put itself in His place. The incident was the inspiration for the two books that contain Nietzsche's best aphorisms, *The Gay Science* and *Thus Spoke Zarathustra*, and even provided Nietzsche with a symbol of how aphorisms themselves work:

Whoever writes in blood and aphorisms does not want to be read but to be learned by heart. In the mountains the shortest way is from peak to peak: but for that one must have long legs. Aphorisms should be peaks – and those who are addressed tall and lofty.

Aphorisms are definitely peak experiences, but Nietzsche's leaps can often be something of a stretch. In all his books, but especially in *Thus Spoke Zarathustra*, Nietzsche writes with an overwhelming bombastic exuberance. His ideas erupt in brilliant and bewildering outbursts; the prose still glows molten red around the edges, but with a few too many purple flares.

In *The Gay Science*, Nietzsche called himself a 'daredevil of the spirit' and he is indeed the Evel Knievel of nineteenth-century philosophy. He jumps recklessly from thought to thought, but crashes and burns as often as he makes it across. Still, for sheer verve, Nietzsche is unparalleled. And anyway, he'd already anticipated his critics, leaving specific instructions for the treatment of those unable or unwilling to follow him:

He whom you cannot teach to fly, teach to fall faster!

Apart from Schopenhauer, Nietzsche's biggest influences were the seventeenth-century French aphorists, particularly Chamfort, Montaigne and La Rochefoucauld. He read these authors intensively and shared their contempt for social convention, moral hypocrisy and received wisdom. In fact, Nietzsche is much more a moralist in the tradition of his French predecessors than he is a systematic thinker like Schopenhauer.

Nietzsche never even tried to create a logically coherent body of thought. His sole aim was to expose and decry the flimsy illusions and self-serving delusions he believed ruled most people's lives. His main target was Christianity, which he said stunted spiritual growth by imposing moral straitjackets and suffocating doctrines on its followers. Nietzsche's aphorisms are passionate exhortations to discard such outmoded beliefs, to break free by recognizing that the human imagination is the true measure of all things:

Good and evil are the prejudices of God.

Nietzsche's 'gay science' of liberation – so called because he thought derisive laughter was the only proper response to restrictive creeds: 'Not by wrath does one kill but by laughter. Come, let us kill the spirit of gravity!' – has a parallel in the dismal science of economics. In the early 1920s, the Czech economist Joseph A. Schumpeter developed the theory of 'creative destruction', which states that economic growth occurs when mature industries and old ways of doing business are eliminated by innovation. A new product or technical advance by one company leaves more complacent firms unable to compete and eventually leads to their destruction.

There's been a lot of creative destruction around since the arrival of the Internet. The ubiquity of e-mail, for example, has largely wiped out what was once a core element of the postal service business: letters. But at the same time, the demand for courier services has increased as more people shop online and have products delivered to their homes and offices. When creative destruction rules, some industries die; others are transformed; and still others are born. Schumpeter argued that entrepreneurs are essential to economic growth because only they dare disrupt the status quo to challenge conventional business models.

Nietzsche was an entrepreneur of the imagination. His innovation was to proclaim that each person alone was the sole arbiter of truth. To reach new spiritual and artistic heights, he knew he had to tear down old beliefs:

**Whoever must be a creator always annihilates.**

In place of those fallen idols, Nietzsche held up the individual. He exulted in breaking barriers, treading on taboos and confounding expectations. By testing and exceeding our own personal limits, Nietzsche believed society's horizons were expanded and enriched. That was the way civilizations innovated. The greatest sin in this new religion of the self was complacency, and the only commandment – think for thyself:

One repays a teacher badly if one always remains nothing but a pupil.

Nietzsche's health began to deteriorate in the late 1870s, and he resorted to a variety of narcotics to ease the pain. He had a nervous breakdown in Turin in January 1889 and was taken back to Germany to live with his family. There his madness finally won him the celebrity he'd been denied during his sane life. Nietzsche's sister Elisabeth took control of his literary affairs and dressed him up in a white robe to exhibit him to tourists as the mad prophet. His books, which had never sold well, now flew off the shelves.

Nietzsche's aphorisms are calls from the wild fringes of philosophy. He praised whatever challenged our most cherished assumptions and condemned whatever deflected the spirit from itself. His aphorisms encourage us to become laws unto ourselves through a perpetual process of creative destruction:

The secret for harvesting from existence the greatest fruitfulness and the greatest enjoyment is – to live dangerously! Build your cities on the slopes of Vesuvius! Send your ships into uncharted seas! Live at war with your peers and yourselves!

## Ludwig Wittgenstein (1889–1951)
### The Outer Limits of Language

'God has arrived. I met him on the 5:15 train.' That's the way economist John Maynard Keynes described Ludwig Wittgenstein's return to Cambridge University in 1929. Wittgenstein's first sojourn in Cambridge began in 1911, when he appeared unannounced outside Bertrand Russell's rooms at Trinity College. The young Austrian had been studying aeronautics in Manchester, but after reading Russell's book *The Principles of Mathematics* dropped his plans for a career in engineering and decided to take up philosophy. In his typically brusque, self-confident manner, Wittgenstein – who at that point had read only sporadically in philosophy – simply showed up at the office of one of the most eminent thinkers on the planet and expected to be taken on as a student.

Russell found Wittgenstein an intense, unnerving and exasperating person – during one discussion on the limits of empirical knowledge, he tried and failed to get Wittgenstein to admit there wasn't a rhinoceros in the room – but allowed him to sit in on his lectures anyway. The two men, along with Keynes and a handful of other Cambridge luminaries, eventually became colleagues and close friends.

Wittgenstein was as brilliant as he was intransigent, and his fierce, uncompromising personality and highly original ideas quickly won him a cult following. With the publication of *Tractatus Logico-Philosophicus* in 1922, the only one of Wittgenstein's works to appear in his lifetime, he acquired such

133

a mystique of genius that Keynes could sardonically equate his return to Cambridge with the Second Coming.

Wittgenstein was a profoundly spiritual man, an odd combination of mendicant and mathematician. He was born into one of the wealthiest and most highly cultured families in Habsburg Vienna. His father was a leading iron and steel magnate who loved music; Brahms and Mahler were regular guests at musical evenings in the Wittgenstein home. Wittgenstein's brother Paul was a concert pianist who lost his right arm in the First World War. He continued with his performing career, though, and in 1931 Ravel composed the *Concerto for the Left Hand* for him.

But Ludwig never quite fitted the mould his parents had in mind for him. He loved crime fiction, devouring each new issue of *Detective Story Magazine*, and Hollywood B-movies, particularly westerns and musicals. He never learned to play an instrument but was a virtuoso whistler. In 1914, he renounced his inheritance and gave what money he had at the time to the editor of a small but influential literary journal on the condition that the funds be distributed among struggling Austrian artists in need of financial assistance. The poets Rainer Maria Rilke and Georg Trakl were two beneficiaries of Wittgenstein's largesse.

From that point on, Wittgenstein led a frugal, ascetic existence, living off the stipend he received from Cambridge and whatever he earned from his periodic employment outside the university. After *Tractatus* was published, he renounced philosophy, too, and left Cambridge to teach in elementary schools in rural Austria. Even after his return to academic life in 1929,

Wittgenstein always tried to dissuade students from pursuing philosophy, urging them instead to take up more useful work, even manual labour:

Just improve yourself; that is the only thing you can do to better the world.

Wittgenstein practised what he preached. Throughout his life, he periodically took jobs outside the teaching profession. During the Second World War, for example, he worked as an orderly at Guy's Hospital in London. But he never stopped developing his philosophy. After the First World War, he abandoned work on logic and mathematics to focus more on metaphysics, ethics, aesthetics and especially the philosophy of language.

Wittgenstein believed

Philosophical problems arise when language goes on holiday.

For him, speculation about the great mysteries of ethics, aesthetics and spirituality was useless, not because these subjects are unimportant but because language isn't capable of saying anything meaningful about them. We can never get to the bottom of a problem, he thought, because we continually hit the boundaries of language, which bounce us back into dead-end debates about abstractions such as whether truth is identical to beauty. Wittgenstein was convinced that when language hits its limits, it becomes impossible to even ask sensible questions, much less to answer them:

What can be said at all can be said clearly, and what we cannot talk about we must pass over in silence.

Think of a piece of music. It doesn't matter whether it's jazz, classical or rock. Now try to describe it. What can you say? Perhaps the trumpet wails plaintively; the violins swell in a lush crescendo; the power chords crash over the primordial thrum of the bass. You can say all this and more and still say absolutely nothing about the music itself. The only way to know a piece of music is to hear it for yourself.

For Wittgenstein, philosophy was a lot like describing a piece of music: impossible. So instead of devising grand metaphysical systems, he tried to make the nature of language – and therefore, thought – clearer, a process he described as 'tidying up a room'. Once the room was nice and tidy – in other words, once language was neatly arranged within its proper limits – he believed so-called philosophical problems would vanish. The task of philosophy was not to solve these problems with big ideas, but to continually reveal them as insoluble:

Philosophy is not a body of doctrine but an activity.

Wittgenstein took Spinoza's axiomatic style to a new extreme. He was a slow, meticulous writer, often adducing startling similes in support of his statements but never providing any background reasoning or evidence. His books are made up solely of terse declarative sentences. Each aphorism is its own proof. When Russell chided him for this, Wittgenstein replied that arguments would spoil the beauty of his insights. And he was right. After all, what explanation can be given when:

Uttering a word is like striking a note on the keyboard of the imagination.

Wittgenstein's vatic pronouncements often read more like poetry than philosophy. He possessed a remarkable flair for imagery; he once wrote that thinking about language was like trying to 'repair a torn spider's web with our fingers'. If he's less convincing as a philosopher than as a poet, perhaps that's because despite all the rigour and precision of his thinking, he was really a mystic at heart, a mystic who took a vow of silence about the things that mattered to him most:

The limits of my language mean the limits of my world.

## E. M. Cioran (1911–95)
### Knight of the Living Dead

As a child, E. M. Cioran loved to loiter in the local cemetery, playing with the human skulls the caretaker would give him. Even as an adult, he retained a fondness for this macabre pastime. 'In the days when I set off on month-long bicycle trips across France,' he wrote, 'my greatest pleasure was to stop in country cemeteries, to stretch out between two graves, and to smoke for hours on end. I think of those days as the most active period of my life.' Perhaps that's why Cioran's aphorisms have such a whiff of death about them:

To live is to lose ground.

Or maybe it's because he was born in Rasinari, a tiny hamlet in the Carparthian mountains of Transylvania, birthplace of one of Romania's greatest legends: Dracula. Perhaps Cioran inherited his dour disposition from his parents, both of whom were intensely religious. His father was a minister in the Romanian Orthodox Church and his mother seems to have been consumed by an all-pervasive sense of spiritual foreboding, a trait shared by her son. Whatever the reason, Cioran was clearly not a happy man. The one thing that seems to have provided some respite from his gloomy musings was writing, though even that offered only temporary relief:

A book is a postponed suicide.

As a young man in the 1930s, Cioran held pretty dismal political views, too. After becoming involved in Romanian far-right politics, he worked for a time as a journalist in Germany, writing articles in praise of the Nazi cult of power. He eventually became a kind of Romanian Ezra Pound, penning fascist political tracts and broadcasting propaganda for the pro-Hitler Romanian government during the early years of the Second World War.

But Cioran's politics changed when he was in his late twenties. He abruptly left Romania and moved to Paris, where he not only renounced his far-right views but the language in which he had expressed them, too. Yet his mood didn't brighten from living in the City of Light. His aphorisms remained as morose as ever; he just wrote them in French.

Cioran was a lifelong fan of Nietzsche, though he could never bring himself to embrace the German philosopher's robust enthusiasms. And like Schopenhauer, Cioran was a devoted student of Buddhism, no doubt because the idea of extinguishing the self appealed to him. But Buddhism is an exuberant, life-affirming practice, qualities Cioran lacked. Unlike Nietzsche and Schopenhauer, though, Cioran was a brooder rather than a thinker and his aphorisms are relentlessly dark little odes to dejection:

This very second has vanished for ever, lost in the anonymous mass of the irrevocable. It will never return. I suffer from this, and I do not. Everything is unique – and insignificant.

In Paris, Cioran lived modestly in a Left Bank attic apartment, earning money as a translator and manuscript reader for publishing houses. He suffered from chronic insomnia, and to escape his sleeplessness would go for long nocturnal strolls in the Luxembourg Gardens. It's said that he often encountered Samuel Beckett there, and that these two great anatomists of modern melancholy would simply nod in silence to one another as they passed. It seems a fitting greeting for writers to whom silence was so golden – and for Cioran, an eloquent statement of his bleak philosophy:

Only one thing matters: learning to be the loser.

# 5 The lack of money is the root of all evil:

## *The Rise of the American One-liner*

Benjamin Franklin was a man of many firsts. He founded the first public library, the first volunteer fire brigade, the first fire insurance company and the first free hospital in the United States. He was the first to demonstrate that lightning was a form of electricity, the first to identify positive and negative electrical currents, and the first to differentiate materials that did conduct electricity from those that didn't. He invented the first bifocal glasses, the first clean-burning stove and the first lightning rod. In 1751, twenty-five years before he helped write the Declaration of Independence, he was the first to suggest that the British colonies in America band together in a confederation to look after their common interests. And beginning in 1732, with the first edition of *Poor Richard's Almanack*, Benjamin Franklin became America's first home-grown aphorist.

Samuel Johnson once quipped:

No man but a blockhead ever wrote except for money.

Benjamin Franklin was no blockhead. In the eighteenth century, almanacs were a crucial source of income for printers because they had to be reissued every year in order to update the meteorological and astronomical information. Franklin had been a printer since his early twenties, but in 1732 he quarrelled with his partner, who left to set up a rival shop, taking the almanac-printing business with him. Without an annual almanac, Franklin faced a potentially catastrophic loss of revenue. So what did the twenty-six-year-old Franklin do? He wrote and printed an almanac at his own expense.

Franklin penned his almanac under the pseudonym of Richard Saunders, an impoverished, absent-minded astrologer who took up writing to make ends meet. In addition to the standard horoscopes, weather predictions and lists of everything from county fairs to solar eclipses, 'Poor Richard' offered his own commonsense musings about how to live a virtuous life and how to earn a living. He intended the almanac to be a source of practical information as well as a 'vehicle for conveying instruction among the common folk', a book studded with tips that 'inculcated industry and frugality as the means of procuring wealth, and thereby securing virtue'. It was another of Franklin's firsts: America's original self-help book.

Poor Richard's sayings have become a kind of aphoristic alphabet every American can recite:

He that lieth down with dogs shall rise up with fleas.

It is hard for an empty sack to stand upright.

141

Little strokes fell great oaks.

Take counsel in wine, but resolve afterwards in water.

Even in Franklin's own day, *Poor Richard's Almanack* was a resounding commercial success. Annual sales of the books not only rescued Franklin from his immediate financial difficulties but remained a source of income and fame for the next quarter-century. When the last edition of the almanac appeared in 1758, Franklin compiled all of Poor Richard's dictums into a single speech, which he published separately as *The Way to Wealth*. This brief essay on the virtues of thrift and hard work was an instant hit, going through more than one hundred editions over the next fifty years. Franklin was first again, this time as America's earliest literary celebrity.

Despite his status as a pioneering aphorist, Franklin was not always original, as he himself confessed. He often borrowed, adapted or simply condensed old English proverbs, or plundered Dryden, Swift, Sterne and Pope, to come up with Poor Richard's encomiums to self-improvement. But the wit and civic spirit that imbue Franklin's aphorisms are entirely his own.

Franklin was Confucius with a sense of humour, La Rochefoucauld with a social conscience. He was a pragmatic civic reformer who believed that the way to do well in the world was to do good, and he was a fearsome social critic who despised pretentiousness, dishonesty and venality. He was, in fact, very much like his great German contemporary, Georg Christoph Lichtenberg. Both were renowned as scientists and wits; both edited almanacs; both won fame for their experiments with electricity; and neither could abide dogmatism in morality or religion:

Different sects like different clocks may all be near the matter, 'tho they don't quite agree.

In his autobiography, Franklin recounts how in 1734, at the age of twenty-eight, he compiled a list of the thirteen essential virtues he considered 'necessary or desirable, and annexed to each a short precept, which fully expressed the extent I gave to its meaning'. Franklin's thirteen commandments include the usual suspects – temperance, cleanliness, humility – and his familiar exhortations to industry and frugality. But there are some surprises as well. Virtue number 2, for example, is silence:

Speak not but what may benefit others or yourself; avoid trifling conversation.

And virtue number 4 is resolution:

Resolve to perform what you ought; perform without fail what you resolve.

This mixture of old-fashioned morality with a newfangled emphasis on self-reliance and personal responsibility became Franklin's aphoristic trademark. He espoused a typically American brand of morality in which the pursuit of spiritual

143

and economic happiness was not only a right but a duty. Franklin was a self-made man, and Poor Richard's maxims were meant to show other people how to find their own ways to wealth. His delivery was typically American, too: blunt, quick and often very funny.

Franklin is the founding father of the American aphorism, and his literary successors all ended up either trying to emulate or subvert him. Some adopted a persona similar to Poor Richard – a simple, homespun character who despite his seeming naivety manages to expose hypocrisy and deceit with wicked one-liners; others embraced Franklin's work ethic and morality but rejected the life of commerce for one of contemplation. But each of Franklin's progeny practised the virtues of industry and self-reliance preached in *Poor Richard's Almanack*; and their aphorisms each follow a rule that Franklin formulated:

The heart of the fool is in his mouth, but the mouth of the wise man is in his heart.

## Ralph Waldo Emerson (1803–82)
### The Prophet of Nonconformity

Mary Moody Emerson had a decisive influence on the intellectual development of her young nephew, Ralph Waldo. She was a small, frail woman with a macabre sense of her own mortality – she slept in a bed shaped like a coffin and wore a burial shroud when travelling. For all her eccentricities, though, she was a fiercely intelligent and deeply religious

144

person who, until her death in 1863, was Emerson's most important spiritual confidante and philosophical sparring partner. 'Always do what you are afraid to do,' she once advised him. Emerson took that counsel to heart, becoming the most iconoclastic thinker in nineteenth-century America.

Emerson inherited his aunt's fascination with death along with her intellectual courage. In March 1832, not long after his twenty-year-old wife died of tuberculosis, Emerson opened up her tomb so he could look inside. He did the same thing in 1857 at the grave of his son Waldo, who had died fifteen years earlier at the age of five.

Emerson always wanted to confront life – and death – face to face. In the journals he began keeping when he was sixteen, he constantly chided himself for dullness, for not working hard enough at his writing, for failing to keep his mind lively and original. 'What is the hardest task in the world?' he asked in one entry, concluding: 'To think.'

Emerson referred to his journals as his 'savings bank'. Like Lichtenberg's 'waste books', they were repositories for the random observations and reflections from which he drew material for the lectures and essays that contain his greatest aphorisms.

If Franklin was America's original aphorist, Emerson was the country's original aphorism enthusiast. His journals are crammed with quotations culled from his vast and eclectic reading. He loved the Stoics, especially Seneca and Marcus Aurelius, and was among the first Americans to read Confucius in English. He was also deeply influenced by Montaigne and Francis Bacon, the two great essayist-aphorists on whom he modelled himself – and whom he consciously set out to imitate. Like his two illustrious predecessors, Emerson took up the aphoristic essay as his literary form of choice.

In his essays, Emerson exhorted readers to apply Franklin's virtues of self-reliance to the business of living. Emerson's golden rule, however, was not industry or frugality but originality:

Insist on yourself; never imitate.

In the mid-1800s, when Emerson was the country's most famous man of letters, America was in the midst of a social and psychological tumult similar to the counter-culture movement of the 1960s. People were experimenting with alternative lifestyles in progressive New England communes such as Brook Farm and Fruitlands; the Transcendentalists were arguing for the supremacy of spirituality over reason; the abolitionists were campaigning against slavery and for the civil rights of African Americans; and the country's first back-to-nature trend sprung up in response to the Industrial Revolution.

Emerson was intellectually involved in all these developments – indeed, he was widely regarded as the most eminent of the Transcendentalists – but he never actually joined any group. He remained a lone rebel, wary of the comfortable certainty that can settle in when people surround themselves with like-minded individuals:

It is easy in the world to live after the world's opinion; it is easy in solitude to live after our own; but the great man is he who in the midst

of the crowd keeps with perfect sweetness the independence of
solitude.

Emerson soon found that independence of mind was not
always so sweet. Like his father before him, he entered the ministry and became widely known for the eloquence and power
of his sermons. But in his late twenties, he began to question
his faith as his thinking took on an increasingly gnostic tinge.
The most important thing, he believed, was not to follow the
teachings of any organized religion but for each individual to
discover his or her own original and inspired relationship to
God.

The death of his first wife prompted the final break with
conventional Christianity. Realizing he no longer believed that
Jesus' death offered human beings any redemption from sin,
Emerson abandoned his vocation and quit the Church. Yet his
ministry continued. He stopped writing sermons and started
writing essays, which he read aloud to large and enraptured
audiences around the country. His message was as simple as it
was subversive:

God builds his temple in the heart on the ruins of churches and
religions.

On one of Emerson's grand tours through Europe, he
visited Italy and travelled to Mount Vesuvius. He hiked up the
side of the peak and stood on the volcano's rim, close enough
to feel the heat and see the little wisps of steam escaping from
cracks in the earth. The experience impressed him deeply. He

bought a print of Vesuvius in eruption as a memento of the trip; it still hangs in the hallway of his home, now a museum, in Concord, Massachusetts.

For Emerson, Vesuvius was the perfect metaphor for the creative life because true originality – in art as well as in life – comes from turmoil, the constant boiling of new insights and ideas. To insist on yourself, he believed, means to persist with yourself, even when your community, your Church or even your friends put up stiff resistance. Only volcanic convictions can break through centuries of ossified tradition and accreted beliefs. Even at the height of his apostasy, though, Emerson was only following his Aunt Mary's advice, facing his fears by daring to hold his hand in the fire of a mind burning at white heat:

People wish to be settled; only as far as they are unsettled is there any hope for them.

## Henry David Thoreau (1817–62)
### The Columbus of Concord

When I was fifteen, I was arrested under the boardwalk in Ocean City, New Jersey, for possession of marijuana. My cousin, a friend and I had just finished getting high and were halfway up the steps from the beach when we saw the police officer waiting for us. He stood at the top of the stairs, directly above the spot where we had just been smoking pot. The aroma had no doubt given us away. He marched us down under the boardwalk again and made us empty our pockets. I happened to be the one with the bag of weed on my person, so I was the one that got busted.

At the police station, I was treated like a real criminal – handcuffed, strip-searched and deprived of my belt and shoelaces before being placed in a holding cell. Throughout the entire ordeal, two thoughts kept going through my head: How can I prevent my parents from finding out? And what would Henry David Thoreau have done in a situation like this?

I was reading *Walden* and *Civil Disobedience* at the time, and Thoreau's description of the night he spent in jail for refusing to pay his poll tax had made a big impression on me. One day in 1846, Thoreau walked from his cabin out near Walden Pond into Concord, Massachusetts, to pick up a shoe he had left for repair. There he encountered Sam Staples, Concord's constable and tax collector. For the past six years Thoreau had refused to pay his poll tax as a protest against the government's support for slavery. Staples had repeatedly warned Thoreau that sooner or later he would have to pay – Staples even offered to lend him the money – but this time Thoreau again refused. Staples had had enough, so he locked Thoreau up. Word of Thoreau's incarceration spread quickly in the small town, and overnight someone paid his tax bill for him (it's still not clear who). He was released the next morning.

I admired Thoreau's defiance – he was not only an abolitionist but also denounced the government for starting what he considered an imperialist war with Mexico – and I agreed with his argument that breaking an unjust law can sometimes be the just thing to do. Sulking in my cell, it occurred to me that a

149

little civil disobedience of my own would demonstrate my then strongly held belief that smoking pot was not a crime, while at the same time preventing my parents from ever finding out I had been arrested. So when the officer asked for my name and address, I curtly replied: 'Fifth Amendment.'

The police tried various forms of persuasion – from gentle cajoling to exasperated reasoning to outright threats – but I resolutely invoked my right to remain silent. So they put me back in the cell to think about it. I figured they would keep me overnight at most, and I would make up a cover story to explain my disappearance to my parents. Unbeknownst to me, though, my cousin had given the police my address and phone number and my mother was already on her way to pick me up. It was an inglorious end to my first – and so far only – brush with the law, but it gave me some small sense at least of what Thoreau was talking about when he wrote:

Under a government which imprisons any unjustly, the true place for a just man is also a prison.

Thoreau was an omnivorous reader and at one point in *Walden*, the wonderful aphoristic account of his experiment of living alone in the woods, he effuses: 'How many a man has dated a new era in his life from the reading of a book!' *Walden* was such a book for me, the founding document of an exhilarating era of self-discovery.

I was assigned a couple of chapters from *Walden* as part of a secondary school literature class, but the book engrossed me so much that I read the whole thing. In fact, I read it four times consecutively; after finishing one reading, I turned right back to the beginning and started all over again.

I still have that battered old paperback from school. On the cover is a woodcut in autumnal tints of a young man sitting under a tree by the side of a lake. The book's margins are strafed by exclamation points, and long passages on every page are neatly underlined in blue, black, red or purple ink. (The four colours represent the four separate readings.)

I loved *Walden* because in it Thoreau expressed so many of the things I was thinking as an introverted teenager given to heterodox views. He was a great disbeliever in frivolity and artifice, reassuring me that it was all right to be out of step with the pastimes and preoccupations of my peers. As the Industrial Revolution introduced America to the uniformity of mass production, Thoreau insisted on individuality and celebrated difference, encouraging me to escape the bland suburban conveyor belt that funnelled kids like me into pastry-cutter careers. For the two years, two months and two days he lived at Walden Pond, Thoreau was a voice in the wilderness shouting out a message none of us hears often enough:

Be a Columbus to whole new continents and worlds within you, opening new channels, not of trade, but of thought.

Thoreau was twenty-eight when he moved into his one-room cabin near Walden Pond. The date was 4 July 1845; he called it his independence day. He went to live in the woods not because he wanted to be a hermit – Thoreau often walked into town to visit his family, he dined every Sunday with the

151

Emersons, and often had friends out to visit – but because he wanted to get back to nature, to get down to basics. He started with the most basic thing of all: building a place to live. 'Near the end of March, 1845,' he wrote, 'I borrowed an axe and went down to the woods by Walden Pond, nearest to where I intended to build my house, and began to cut down some tall arrowy white pines, still in their youth, for timber. It is difficult to begin without borrowing.'

What Thoreau never acknowledged in *Walden* was that he borrowed more than just an axe; the land on which he built, along with the very idea of living out by the pond in the first place, were borrowed from Ralph Waldo Emerson.

Emerson and Thoreau first met in 1837 in Concord, when Thoreau was a twenty-year-old undergraduate at Harvard and Emerson was thirty-four and already famous. Thoreau visited the Emerson household often. He periodically lived there, too, especially when Emerson himself was off on lecture tours or travelling in Europe. Thoreau became a kind of surrogate big brother to Emerson's three young children.

The two men had a close relationship, alternating between warm friendship and intense rivalry. Thoreau felt privileged to be the friend of such an eminent writer, and Emerson savoured Thoreau's energy and wit. Once, when Emerson remarked that Harvard taught all the branches of learning, Thoreau shot back: 'Yes, indeed, all the branches and none of the roots.'

The exchange is indicative of both men's characters. Emerson was an unconventional thinker who lived a very conventional life. Though he rejected Christianity and preached nonconformity, he somehow remained an Establishment figure and a pillar of New England society. Thoreau, on the other hand, was far less original in his thinking but lived a highly unconventional life. He never held a steady job, never married, never raised a family. In many ways, he practised what Emerson preached. Emerson dreamed of building a little cabin on the land he bought near Walden Pond, but it was Thoreau who actually did it.

Yet Emerson was essential to Thoreau's development as both a person and a writer. In addition to lending him the land and the idea of moving to the woods, Emerson was also the one who counselled Thoreau to keep a journal of his sojourn at the pond. And it's that journal which eventually became *Walden*, Thoreau's majestic manifesto of the kind of life worth living, whether in the woods, the city or the suburbs:

I went to the woods because I wished to live deliberately, to front only the essential facts of life, and see if I could not learn what it had to teach, and not, when I came to die, discover that I had not lived.

That may sound hopelessly idealistic, even quaint, today, but Thoreau was no utopian fantasist or idle dreamer. On the contrary, he was America's hardest-working, most practically minded philosopher, the very embodiment of Emerson's call for self-reliance and Franklin's exhortation to industry.

As a young man, Thoreau hoped to establish a career as a schoolteacher. But he abandoned that plan after just two weeks; his superiors demanded that he cane his students, the

153

usual form of discipline at the time, and Thoreau refused. Instead of giving up, though, he and his brother started their own school, which thrived for a time but eventually closed down for lack of pupils.

Thoreau then started work at his father's pencil factory. Though he dreaded the drudgery, he nevertheless managed to develop a new type of grinding mill and a smoother lead mixture, both of which greatly enhanced the quality of the pencils. But the cabin at Walden Pond was the most eloquent statement of Thoreau's do-it-yourself spirit, proof of his view that even the loftiest thoughts mean little unless they're applied in daily life:

If you have built castles in the air, your work need not be lost; that is where they should be. Now put the foundations under them.

Emerson was America's Seneca – distinguished, wise, avuncular; Thoreau was its Diogenes – blunt, disdainful, confrontational. Like Diogenes, Thoreau wanted to live honestly and simply, unencumbered by conventional possessions or expectations. And like a true Stoic, he found his model for the enlightened life in nature: his own nature as well as the natural world around him. His only rule was to be true to yourself, whatever the cost:

If a man does not keep pace with his companions, perhaps it is because he hears a different drummer. Let him step to the music which he hears, however measured or far away.

154

Thoreau's health was always precarious, and at the age of forty-four he caught a severe cold after one of his frequent walks in the woods. The cold became tuberculosis. When it was clear Thoreau wouldn't recover, his Aunt Louisa asked whether he had made his peace with God. 'I did not know we had ever quarrelled,' Thoreau replied.

## Mark Twain (1835–1910)
### The Merry Misanthrope

Samuel Langhorne Clemens was born in Florida, Missouri, and moved to Hannibal – home of Huck Finn and Tom Sawyer – when he was four. He didn't adopt his pseudonym, Mark Twain, until 1863. His life had some striking parallels with that of another American aphorist, a man whose rough, homespun persona Twain adopted but whose philosophy he relentlessly parodied – Benjamin Franklin.

Twain and Franklin both got into the printing business at an early age; Twain became a printer's apprentice at the Hannibal *Gazette*, and for a while even worked at the Philadelphia *Inquirer* in Franklin's old stomping grounds. Both men were seasoned travellers; Franklin spent a good part of his later life in England and France as a representative of the new American government, while Twain lived in London and Vienna, took a trip through the Middle East and made a round-the-world lecture tour in 1895/96. Both loved technology and were enthusiastic inventors; Twain was nowhere near as prolific as Franklin but he did devise the 'elastic strap', a prototype of

155

what would one day become suspenders, and the self-pasting scrapbook, one of the earliest photo albums. And both shared a love of money-making schemes; Franklin made a fortune from his shrewd investments while Twain . . . well, sadly, there the similarities end.

Twain never met a dodgy business proposition he didn't like. He was infatuated by technology and easily seduced by promises of instant wealth. He bought one of the first typewriters in America; the manuscript of *Life on the Mississippi* was perhaps the first book to be typed instead of written out by hand. He attended an early demonstration of the telephone, too, and had one of the first private phones in the country installed in his home in Hartford, Connecticut, in 1877. The phone connected him directly to the offices of the Hartford *Courant* newspaper, and can still be seen in Twain's house, now a museum.

But Twain displayed disastrously bad judgement when it came to investing his often considerable book royalties. He was urged to buy stock in Alexander Graham Bell's company, for example, but he didn't. Instead, he poured his money into things such as 'plasmon', a food additive extracted from dairy waste that never made it to market; new machines for book-engraving, typesetting and carpet-weaving, all of which failed, as did his scheme for a steam-powered whisky still; and the Independent Watch Company of Fredonia, a business that never actually existed. Twain ended up earning and losing several fortunes in his lifetime, a predicament that undoubtedly led him to conclude:

156

The lack of money is the root of all evil.

Twain and Franklin shared a healthy appreciation for the acquisition of wealth, but in practically every other respect the two men were complete opposites. Twain called Franklin 'the immortal axiom-builder, who used to sit up nights reducing the rankest old threadbare platitudes to crisp and snappy maxims that had a nice, varnished, original look in their regimentals'. Twain deliberately set out to overturn Franklin's friendly, avuncular sayings with his own darker, more ornery aphorisms.

Though Twain's literary persona – a gruff, plain-talking 'innocent' – was simply a Southern version of Poor Richard, he wanted to be the anti-Franklin in everything. While Franklin urged a strong work ethic:

Early to bed, and early to rise, makes a man healthy, wealthy, and wise

Twain praised procrastination:

Do not put off till tomorrow what can be put off till day-after-tomorrow just as well.

And while Franklin counselled the importance of right action:

A good example is the best sermon

Twain found any instance of upright behaviour insufferable:

157

Few things are harder to put up with than the annoyance of a good example.

After he was rescued from drowning several times as a boy, Twain came to believe he led a charmed life. And in many ways, he did. During his days as a river-boat pilot on the Mississippi in the late 1850s, Twain was scheduled to do a stint on a boat called the *Pennsylvania*. But his brother, Henry, offered to swap postings and Twain readily agreed. A few days later, a fire broke out on the *Pennsylvania* and the boat exploded. Henry was killed, and Twain spent the rest of his life haunted by the thought that he could have – perhaps should have – been in his brother's place.

At the beginning of the Civil War, Twain briefly joined a ragtag Confederate militia. But apart from some desultory marching towards and away from rumoured Union troop concentrations, he didn't see any action. In 1861, he went to Nevada to try his luck in the gold rush. Naturally, he failed. After that, he became a reporter for a variety of Nevada newspapers, writing satirical sketches and short pieces of fiction that were parodies of real events and people. When the recipients of Twain's satire started getting upset, and litigious, Twain's editor suggested he might want to consider a pseudonym. Thus, Mark Twain was born.

Twain found his forte as a journalist; it was the only job he was ever really good at. He began as a combination of columnist and travel writer, penning witty letters and sketches from various exotic locations both inside and outside the United States. He later worked these pieces up into his first book, *The*

*Innocents Abroad*, which became a major success. As his books and journalism flourished, Twain hit the road on the nineteenth-century equivalent of the stand-up comedy circuit. He gave public lectures and humorous talks all around the country, and his mop of curly hair, bushy white moustache and ever-present cigar became instantly recognizable everywhere.

Twain's aphorisms are always cantankerous and contrarian. He had a very low tolerance of common sense, conventional morality and religious piety. His wife, Olivia, who came from an extremely devout (and wealthy) Christian family, spent the early part of their marriage labouring to bring Twain back into the fold. But instead of converting Twain, she ended up losing her own faith. Twain saw it as just more evidence that:

The altar-cloth of one aeon is the door-mat of the next.

One thing Twain never lost faith in, though, was the power of humour. His most successful novels are comedies of manners, anti-morality tales in which he skewers the pretensions and pomposities of people from all walks of life and all social classes. Towards the end of his life, Twain became increasingly disaffected with politics, too. He was particularly scathing about what he considered American imperialism in Cuba and the Philippines after the Spanish-American War. He wrote a broadside decrying the appalling treatment of African Americans in the country, but declined to publish it for fear that a public backlash would hurt sales of his other books. The imperatives of Twain's conscience didn't always prevail over those of his wallet, but his aphorisms are powerful reminders that wit can be a lethal weapon:

Irreverence is the champion of liberty, and its only sure defence.

For a man who believed he led a charmed life, Twain had a remarkable ability to see the worst in every situation. Though his misanthropic view of the world became more severe and sinister in his later years, there's always something frolicsome about even his darkest musings, as if he regarded the journey from birth to death as just one vast practical joke. Even when delivering his dismal final verdict on life, Twain couldn't resist one last prank:

The first half of it consists of the capacity to enjoy without the chance; the last half consists of the chance without the capacity.

## Ambrose Bierce (1842–1914?)
Lucifer's Lexicographer

Marcus Aurelius Bierce was a peculiar person. A failed businessman and successful religious zealot, he was passionate about literature and amassed one of America's largest private libraries in one of its unlikeliest places – the obscure town of Warsaw, Indiana. He insisted on giving all of his thirteen offspring names beginning with the letter A. By the time baby number ten arrived, Ambrose was one of the few boys' names left.

As a child, Ambrose Bierce nurtured his love of literature in his father's library. As a young man, he followed a career path very similar to Mark Twain's. He became a printer's assistant in his early teens and when the Civil War broke out he enlisted in the Union army. Unlike Twain, though, Bierce fought in some of the conflict's bloodiest engagements, including the battles of Shiloh and Chickamauga. He was wounded several times, once taking a bullet in the head. He came to despise the incompetence and venality of his commanding officers, and the war's carnage only confirmed his already saturnine view of the human condition.

After resigning his commission in 1865, Bierce wandered around the American frontier for a couple of years in the hope of making his fortune. He briefly tried his hand at mining in South Dakota, with disastrous results, and ended up marooned and penniless in San Francisco. There he fell into a job on a local newspaper writing short essays and editorials exposing hypocrisy and corruption among the city's great and good. He quickly made his name as California's fiercest crusading journalist – attacking craven politicians, taking on the state's robber barons, defending the rights of minorities such as the Chinese – and defined his political and social agenda like this:

My future program will be calm disapproval of human institutions in general, including all forms of government, most laws and customs, and all contemporary literature; enthusiastic belief in the Darwinian theory, intolerance of intolerance, and war upon every man with a mission . . . human suffering and human injustice in all their forms to be contemplated with a merely curious interest, as one looks into an anthill.

In 1880, Bierce melded this anthropological approach with his satanic sense of humour in a new column for *The Wasp* newspaper called 'The Devil's Dictionary'. Over the next thirty years, he delighted readers with his diabolical definitions of everything from abasement to zoology, eventually giving his own twisted, aphoristic meanings to over a thousand different words. Bierce's lexicon of human misery is bilious, mordant and hilarious, as in the following typical entry:

Misfortune, n. The kind of fortune that never misses.

Bierce adopted an appropriately satanic persona to match his new literary style. He dressed in black, carried a revolver (for self-defence against his many enemies, he claimed), and displayed a human skull and a box of ashes on his desk. He saw himself as continuing the great tradition of satirical dictionaries pioneered by the likes of Samuel Johnson and Gustave Flaubert, and was quick to take issue with his illustrious predecessors when he disagreed about a specific meaning. Bierce took Dr Johnson to task, for example, about what's become the latter's most famous definition:

Patriotism, n. Combustible rubbish ready to the torch of anyone ambitious to illuminate his name. In Dr Johnson's famous dictionary patriotism is defined as the last refuge of a scoundrel. With all due respect to an enlightened but inferior lexicographer I beg to submit that it is the first.

Bierce was extremely generous with his scorn. Cant and sham roused his greatest fury, with businessmen, politicians and the clergy the most frequent recipients of his wrath. Like La Rochefoucauld, he believed human beings were instinctively selfish, disingenuous and untrustworthy. Those who held the greatest convictions were worthy of the greatest suspicion:

Self-evident, adj. Evident to one's self and to nobody else.

Bierce's experiences during the Civil War, as well as the poverty and injustice he witnessed in the wild American west, convinced him that conventional morality was a fraud. People would, he believed, do just about anything given the chance to make a profit. All the Sunday sermons and political platitudes in the world couldn't disguise the fact that in pursuit of the American dream, it was every man for himself:

Back, n. That part of your friend which it is your privilege to contemplate in your adversity.

When he wasn't penning his perfidious definitions, Bierce wrote gruesome war stories and supernatural tales of lurid murders, premature burials and unexplained disappearances, like a slightly less cerebral Edgar Allan Poe. One of his favourite plot devices was to have the main character commit suicide. Death was a more or less constant topic of meditation for Bierce, and both his short stories and his aphorisms are infused with starkly beautiful funereal imagery:

Oblivion, n. The state or condition in which the wicked cease from struggling and the dreary are at rest. Fame's eternal dumping ground. Cold storage for high hopes. A place where ambitious authors meet their works without pride and their betters without envy. A dormitory without an alarm clock.

In 1913, at the age of seventy-one, Bierce decided to apply his favourite plot device to his own life. After making a tour of the Civil War battlefields in West Virginia and Tennessee where he had fought, Bierce wrote a handful of letters to friends and relatives informing them that he planned to visit Mexico, which was then in the throes of a violent revolution. He apparently did go to Mexico – or at least several letters signed by him with Mexican postmarks were received by friends – but Bierce himself was never seen again. He just vanished, like a character in one of his short stories.

Within a few weeks of Bierce's disappearance, rumours began circulating that he was actually a secret government agent sent to Mexico to spy on the Germans and the Japanese, who were alleged to be planning an invasion of the USA from the south. Other theories held that he had been killed in battle while fighting alongside revolutionary leader Pancho Villa or that he faked his own death and fled to South America. As late as the 1930s, an explorer was said to have encountered a strange white man clad in jaguar skins (presumably Bierce) in the Brazilian jungle, where the local tribe worshipped him as a god.

As entertaining as these theories are, the more likely explanation is that Bierce arranged the illusory Mexican expedition as a diversion from his true intention: to go to the Grand Canyon to commit suicide. It was an idea he had mentioned, seemingly in jest, to friends on several occasions. But as he grew older and more disgusted with life, he may have reasoned that it would be better to end things on his own terms in a place that he loved. Whatever the truth, Bierce's body was never found – not in Mexico, South America or the Grand Canyon.

Bierce once described his definitions as 'laughorisms'. Indeed, there is a humour in his aphorisms but it is exceedingly black, as befits a man who found this the worst of all possible worlds. Given his dark appraisal of human nature, Bierce's mysterious disappearance and presumed suicide brought to a fitting end a long, strange trip that the lexicographer himself would no doubt have considered pointless:

Road, n. A strip of land along which one may pass from where it is too tiresome to be to where it is futile to go.

# 6 Know then thyself, presume not God to scan; the proper study of mankind is man:

## In Praise of Light Verse

Edward Fitzgerald, the nineteenth-century English dilettante and amateur botanist, was a great collector of aphorisms but, unfortunately, not much of an aphorist himself. In 1852, he published *Polonius: A Collection of Wise Saws and Modern Instances*, a selection of some of his original sayings but mostly a compendium of those of his favourite authors, who included Seneca, Goethe, Jonathan Swift and Francis Bacon. Fitzgerald's own aphorisms are pretty turgid stuff, filled with a faux classicism that strikes the modern reader as annoyingly contrived. But Fitzgerald nevertheless played a pivotal role in the history of the form, at that point where the aphorism intersects with the popular, easily accessible style of poetry known as 'light verse'.

Fitzgerald lived the life of a country squire in Suffolk. His parents were members of the landed gentry and owned several estates in England and Ireland. Though he was friends with famous authors such as William Thackeray and Alfred Tennyson, Fitzgerald avoided literary London to lead a quiet, secluded life near the town of Woodbridge. Since he didn't need to work, he occupied himself with the study of flowers, music and literature. In his mid-forties, Fitzgerald started to learn Persian to pursue an interest in Near Eastern spirituality, and as part of his research stumbled across the writings of an obscure twelfth-century mystical poet named Omar Khayyam.

Khayyam was born in the little town of Naishapur in what is now Iran. Few facts have been established about his life, but he may have followed his father into the tent-making business (the word *khayyam* means 'tent-maker') while also studying astronomy and mathematics. He wrote a number of important mathematical treatises and eventually became Sultan Malik Shah's personal astronomer. But Khayyam was also a poet, and it was his *Rubaiyat* which Fitzgerald discovered in the course of his Persian studies.

Fitzgerald was fascinated by the way Khayyam mixed the mundane with the mystical in his poetry, and he set about translating the *Rubaiyat* (which means 'a collection of rhymes') into English quatrains. On 15 January 1859, he anonymously published a pamphlet called *The Rubaiyat of Omar Khayyam* containing seventy-five of his very freely translated versions. Fitzgerald and Khayyam were almost equally unknown at the time, so Fitzgerald had to pay for the publication himself.

The book received absolutely no notice whatsoever when it first appeared, and quickly ended up in the remaindered stacks of London's second-hand bookshops – which is where the poet and painter Dante Gabriel Rossetti found a copy in 1860. Rossetti was charmed by Khayyam's sensuous, spiritual verse and impressed by Fitzgerald's rhythmic, rhyming translations. He urged his influential literary friends to scour London for copies of the *Rubaiyat* and slowly – largely by word of mouth – the book became a classic.

To this day, it's practically impossible to browse through any second-hand bookstore without encountering a copy of the *Rubaiyat*. There must be hundreds of different editions in existence, many sporting wonderfully garish colour illustrations of a young bearded philosopher (or sometimes an old one) reclining on some plush divan surrounded by a clutch of nubile young women invariably cradling lutes and wine flasks. Like Rossetti, I discovered the *Rubaiyat* by chance – a mouldy, water-damaged old edition from 1947 in the poetry section of a used bookshop. I loved the outlandish illustrations and was immediately entranced by Fitzgerald's deft renditions of Khayyam's paeans to the *carpe diem* spirit:

Here with a loaf of bread beneath the bough,
A flask of wine, a book of verse – and thou
Beside me singing in the wilderness –
And wilderness is paradise enow.

All great light verse gives off an aphoristic illumination; it's bright and playful but also scorching. Like aphorisms, light verse may come across as lightweight on first reading – clever and funny but ultimately not very 'serious'. Yet underneath the surface charms – the comfortable rhymes and reassuring rhythms – there is a scalding wit and an often sulphurous vision.

Since Fitzgerald's translations first made him famous, Khayyam has acquired a reputation as a reckless sybarite, a kind of Persian Epicurus who gleefully discarded the Greek philosopher's emphasis on moderation. While Khayyam did have a proclivity to wine, romance and song, the *Rubaiyat* is more than just a collection of hymns to drunkenness. Khayyam was a philosopher as well as a hedonist. He followed the Stoics in disdaining metaphysics and ridiculing any system of thought or belief that based itself solely on theoretical knowledge:

Myself when young did eagerly frequent
Doctor and saint, and heard great argument
About it and about: but evermore
Came out by the same door as in I went.

Khayyam is capable of far darker strains, too, the kind of grim, vaguely sinister stanzas E. M. Cioran might have composed if he wrote verse:

The moving finger writes; and, having writ,
Moves on: nor all thy piety nor wit
Shall lure it back to cancel half a line,
Nor all thy tears wash out a word of it.

Omar Khayyam – aided and abetted by Edward Fitzgerald – was one of the earliest poet-aphorists, writers whose aphorisms are like gift-wrapped hand grenades: once you tear away the pleasing packaging, you realize you're holding something explosive. The versifiers who came after him turned the aphorism into poetry, using all the tools of prosody to make their searing, subversive stanzas sing. They made the form dance to the music of their times, thereby adding a sixth imperative to the five laws of aphorisms: it must rhyme.

## Alexander Pope (1688–1744)
### The Epic Aphorist

From the seventeenth to the nineteenth centuries, there was an unusually high correlation between poor health and being a great aphorist. Chamfort, Joubert, Nietzsche, Pascal and Vauvenargues all suffered more or less constant bouts of serious illness, as did Lichtenberg and Alexander Pope, both of whom were hunchbacks. When Pope was about eight, he contracted spinal tuberculosis from infected milk. The disease stunted his growth – as an adult, he stood just 4 feet 6 inches tall – and caused a progressive curvature of his spine. He was prone to severe headaches, spasmodic fits and respiratory problems. Towards the end of his life, he was unable to dress himself and had to wear an iron corset just to sit upright. The aphorisms of these men are among the most acerbic in the history of the form, but only Lichtenberg and Pope leavened their vitriol with an equally potent sense of humour.

Pope's joviality was no doubt partly a way of coping with his disability, but it was also due in part to the influence of his literary role models, Erasmus and Montaigne. Like them, Pope was a humanist thinker who believed that human failings should be treated with a modicum of mirth. He rejected all forms of religious and moral dogmatism, advocating instead (in an aphorism that would later be purloined and adapted by Benjamin Franklin) a wry tolerance for human folly:

'Tis with our judgements as our watches, none
Go just alike, yet each believes his own.

Pope is unique in being a writer who composed epic poems – his major works, *An Essay on Criticism*, *An Essay on Man* and *The Dunciad*, are all hundreds of lines long – in which almost every other couplet can stand alone as a distinct aphorism. He had an amazing ability to craft the longest kind of poem from dozens of the shortest kind. Pope is also exceptional for the number of his aphorisms that have already evolved (or degenerated) into proverbs. Many of his classic phrases have entered modern parlance without his name attached. Everyone knows it was Benjamin Franklin who said

A penny saved is a penny earned.

But who remembers that it was Pope who wrote:

A little learning is a dangerous thing.

To err is human, to forgive divine.

Fools rush in where angels fear to tread.

Hope springs eternal in the human breast.

Pope's *An Essay on Man* is perhaps the most quoted and quotable poem in the English language. He wrote it with both a didactic and satiric purpose in mind: it was intended as a statement of his ethical and philosophical system as well as an excoriation of the views with which he disagreed. Pope believed that the world was governed by a divine plan but it was not our lot to understand or even descry it. Our task was not to explain life, the universe and everything but to explore the microcosm that is the self.

Updating Epictetus for the age of enlightenment, Pope argued that life seems cruel and capricious only because we're blind to the grand scheme of things. Therefore, we should grin and bear whatever befalls us knowing that, ultimately, it's not up to us and will, eventually, turn out for the best:

All Nature is but Art, unknown to thee;
All Chance, Direction, which thou canst not see;
All Discord, Harmony, not understood;
All partial Evil, universal Good:
And, spite of Pride, in erring Reason's spite,
One truth is clear, 'Whatever is, is right.'

It's one thing for a pampered Roman Stoic to espouse this view, but it's quite another for Pope, who suffered excruciating pain and discomfort throughout his life. It would have been easy, and pretty understandable, for Pope to feel unfairly victimized by the illness that struck him. He was often reminded of his disability by his many political and literary enemies, who responded to Pope's attacks by ridiculing his appearance.

Things got so tense for a while that Pope is said to have carried a loaded pistol in his pocket whenever he went out, like Ambrose Bierce.

Pope chose to write in tidy, rhyming couplets to make sure his message made a lasting impression. Indeed, his verse has the staying power of a catchy pop tune; once it gets stuck in your head, it's difficult to dislodge. He used aphorisms in his poetry to get to the point swiftly and succinctly. One of his consistent themes is that when it comes to wisdom, all men are created equally dumb and therefore should be equally humble:

In Parts superior what advantage lies?
Tell (for You can) what is it to be wise?
'Tis but to know how little can be known;
To see all others faults, and feel our own.

Pope was an accomplished scholar, and earned a modest fortune from his popular translation of the *Iliad*. He loved classical culture and set out to recreate a little patch of ancient Greece in the grounds of his estate in Twickenham, which in 1719 was a lush little village along the Thames. As an aid to reflection, Pope decided to build under his house a nymphaeum, a cavern or grotto that in Homeric lore was believed to be the home of the muses.

Pope was a skilled and avid gardener and collected rocks and minerals from all over England to adorn his underground museum. During the digging, he discovered a natural spring and fashioned a rivulet that flowed from the cave and emptied into the Thames at the bottom of the garden. Well-travelled

173

friends sent him exotic materials – petrified wood, fossils, bird's nests, coral – all of which Pope carefully affixed to the walls. By the time it was finished, the grotto was encrusted with minerals, shells, shards of mirrored glass and slag from glass furnaces; it was bright with crystalline reflections and awash in the sound of purling waters.

Pope's grotto was so stunning that it became a sightseeing attraction and arrangements had to be made for guided tours. After Pope died, the cavern – now beneath a primary school – became a literary pilgrimage site, attracting visitors from all over the world. Just like tourists in all times and all places, many of these pilgrims took a little piece of the place away with them. Today, visitors will find only bare walls. But there's still something magical about the place, the cave where Pope himself pondered the age-old instructions of the oracle at Delphi:

Know then thyself, presume not God to scan;
The proper study of mankind is man.


## William Blake (1757–1827)
### Poet, Painter, Printer, Prophet

Like the troubled young boy in the film *The Sixth Sense*, William Blake saw dead people. One of his earliest visions came when he was about eight. While walking in the country just outside London, Blake said he saw a tree draped with angels. His mother used to beat him for claiming he'd met the Old Testament prophet Ezekiel and the angel Gabriel. As a young apprentice engraver, Blake had a job sketching the

174

tombs at Westminster Abbey, where he regularly witnessed ghostly processions of medieval monks murmuring plainsong chants. His dead brother Robert was in the habit of passing on new engraving techniques to him from the afterlife. And as an adult, Blake held seances during which he executed quick portraits of some of the great historical figures who came to visit, including King Herod, Michelangelo, Paracelsus, Voltaire and Socrates. Blake was so distracted by his visions that his wife, Catherine, once remarked to an acquaintance: 'I have very little of Mr Blake's company; he is always in Paradise.'

Most people thought Blake was mad, but he believed the visionary company he kept was conclusive proof that we all live surrounded by hosts of spirits, that there is no real division between this world and the next. Blake was both terrified and exhilarated by these spectral visitations, yet he accepted them as evidence of his exuberant faith in the fact that life on earth is a paradise unto itself:

Everything that lives is Holy.

Born above his father's hosier shop in London's Soho, Blake was a recalcitrant child who demonstrated an early aptitude for art, poetry and religious studies. Recognizing his son's unusual talents, his father kept him home from school and excused him from the family business. He also tried to encourage Blake's artistic ambitions by giving him money to purchase cheap prints and engravings for his studies.

Blake's thinking was influenced by the philosopher and mystic Emanuel Swedenborg, who believed that people rose from the dead to inhabit bodies in other worlds. Blake mixed his private visions with Swedenborg's philosophy to devise an elaborate alternative mythology based on the personalities and stories from the Bible but imbued with his own idiosyncratic meanings and symbolism.

Blake was also a fan of Johann Kaspar Lavater, the Swiss scientist and inventor of physiognomy. In 1787, Lavater published a book called *Aphorisms on Man*. (The title page features a familiar epigraph from Pope: 'The proper study of mankind is man'.) Blake found these shrewd reflections on everything from good manners to religious belief inspiring, and scribbled enthusiastic replies to Lavater's aphorisms in his copy of the book, much as G. K. Chesterton would do a hundred and some years later with Holbrook Jackson's *Platitudes in the Making*. Using Lavater as a model, Blake paired his poems – many of which, such as 'The Marriage of Heaven and Hell', are really a string of thematically related aphorisms – with his paintings to create stunning illuminated manuscripts. These little books, which he hand-coloured and printed himself, became bold and dramatic statements of Blake's self-made faith.

Among Blake's earliest aphoristic works is a brief tract called *All Religions Are One*, in which he sets out the gnostic basis of his spirituality: each person must come to his or her revelation alone. On one sheet, below the image of a sole wayfarer walking with a staff in his hand, Blake wrote:

As none by travelling over known lands can find out the unknown. So from already acquired knowledge Man could not acquire more.

176

For Blake, the road less travelled was the only one worth following. He never joined any group or movement, always working alone, with his wife as his sole assistant. He didn't much care what people thought of him, either, shrugging off the scandal caused when he and his wife were observed one summer afternoon sitting naked in their garden reading aloud passages from Milton's *Paradise Lost*. He scorned organized religion and was skilled at losing friends and alienating people owing to his stubborn, pugnacious manner. The only thing that mattered to Blake was finding his own way and sticking to it, however misguided others thought the journey might be:

The road of excess leads to the palace of wisdom.

Blake worked in obscurity and penury all his life, often barely scraping by on the patronage of devoted and sympathetic friends. He could easily have earned more money by putting aside his grand, often monstrous designs in favour of commercially viable works that fitted the popular fashion of the times, such as his early sketches inside Westminster Abbey. He declined because to do so would be to betray his genius, and he refused to sacrifice his inner life just to make a living. Again, most people thought he was crazy. But Blake insisted on himself, making tenacity a prerequisite for enlightenment:

If the fool would persist in his folly he would become wise.

Blake was nothing if not persistent, and the aphorisms and paintings his contemporaries regarded as lunacy are, in fact,

177

eloquent and original testaments to a powerfully felt sense of spirituality. When he rejected conventional religion, Blake replaced it with his personal theology, complete with its own devotional art and sacred scriptures – all of which Blake created himself. He wrote his own gospels, and his good news is that paradise is all around us and salvation consists in simply seeing that fact afresh with our own eyes:

If the doors of perception were cleansed every thing would appear to man as it is, infinite.

## Emily Dickinson (1830–86)
### The Hermit of Amherst

One of the most puzzling questions about the history of the aphorism is why there have been so few female practitioners. Women have, of course, employed the form. In the seventeenth century, Madame de Sablé wrote her own aphorisms as well as revising those of La Rochefoucauld. In the twentieth century, the prose of Gertrude Stein and the poetry of Charlotte Mew are often aphoristic. But male aphorists have always far outnumbered female ones, and Emily Dickinson is the first woman to make a truly exceptional contribution to the form.

Dickinson was born into a prominent family in Amherst, Massachusetts, and spent most of her adult life within the narrow orbit of her home and garden on North Pleasant Street. Like her contemporary and kindred spirit Henry David Thoreau, she was an accomplished naturalist and usually preferred the company of plants and flowers to that of other human beings.

A vivacious and intelligent teenager, she grew increasingly estranged from her friends in her early twenties. As her classmates matured, married businessmen or missionaries, and became pious and respected members of the community, Dickinson withdrew into a private world of books and botany. Her closest confidants became her poetry and her piano, which she is said to have played proficiently.

'If I feel physically as if the top of my head were taken off, I know *that* is poetry.' That's how Dickinson once described her reaction to reading verse. It's an excellent description of the experience of reading her own work, too. Dickinson's poems show the power of light verse to handle the weightiest subjects. Her stanzas are dense and highly strung; like coiled springs, they release tremendous energy when unsprung. And each one has a dizzying aphoristic core that telescopes conventional perspectives and reverses traditional points of view:

Count not that far that can be had,
Though sunset lie between –
Nor that adjacent, that beside,
Is further than the sun.


Dickinson inhabited a world in which the ordinary laws of distance did not apply. She didn't need to retreat to the woods like Thoreau to find solitude. In the midst of busy little Amherst, with her family, friends and neighbours living all around her, she managed to remain thoroughly alone. And though she rarely left the immediate vicinity of her home, she ranged far and wide in her imagination. Just as aphorisms pack a world of meaning into the smallest phrase, Dickinson's poems collapse a universe of human experience into the bounds of her own isolated, mostly uneventful life:

The Life we have is very great.
The Life that we shall see
Surpasses it, we know, because
It is Infinity.
But when all Space has been beheld
And all Dominion shown
The smallest Human Heart's extent
Reduces it to none.

A few physical descriptions of Dickinson survive. One of the most memorable is from Joseph Lyman, a journalist with the *New York Times* who was a frequent visitor to the Dickinson household during the 1860s: 'Enter a spirit clad in white, figure so draped as to be misty, face moist, translucent alabaster, forehead firmer as of statuary marble. Eyes once bright hazel now melted and fused so as to be two dreamy, wondering wells of expression . . . mouth made for nothing and used for nothing but uttering choice speech, rare thoughts, glittering, starry misty figures, winged words.'

This highly romanticized sketch makes Dickinson sound more like a wraith than a smart, introverted woman in her thirties. Descriptions such as this – many of them written while Dickinson's poems were becoming famous but decades after the encounters took place – fed the legends about the hermit of Amherst, who wrote amazing poems but never ventured beyond her front door.

In fact, little is actually known about Dickinson's day-to-day life, mostly because so much of it was lived inside her own mind. Apart from one or two apparently unrequited love affairs, her biography is devoid of any momentous events or turning points. In her letters and manuscripts, she barely mentions the outside world at all, not even something as dramatic as the Civil War, which she lived through. She was very much a world unto herself.

It's impossible to know whether Dickinson's retreat from society was due to her innate shyness, her failed romantic liaisons or something else entirely. Whatever the cause, she never seemed to dread her seclusion. On the contrary, she revelled in it. The most passionate relationship she had was with herself; other ties and obligations would only distract her from it. At roughly the same time that Thoreau was at Walden Pond invoking Columbus as a metaphor for discovering the self, Dickinson was citing another explorer, Hernando de Soto, for the same purpose:

Soto! Explore thyself!
Therein thyself shall find
The 'Undiscovered Continent' –
No Settler has the Mind.

Dickinson pioneered a vast new region of American poetry in which the poet's own thoughts and feelings became the centre of attention. She was less a spinster than a free spirit, a woman unwilling, and perhaps emotionally unable, to live a 'normal' life. Though she led a hermetically sealed existence, her intellect remained expansive and unfettered. Her taut, aphoristic verse is a reminder to all aspiring explorers that, however constrained their own lives might seem, to survive on the frontier you must find within yourself all the sustenance you'll need:

Who goes to dine must take his Feast
Or find the Banquet mean –
The Table is not laid without
Till it is laid within.

## Samuel Hoffenstein (1890–1947)
### Making Light of Dark Times

Six months after it was published in 1928, Samuel Hoffenstein's first book, *Poems in Praise of Practically Nothing*, had sold some 90,000 copies, an astonishingly high figure for a book of poetry. When Hoffenstein died in 1947, sales had reached nearly 200,000, and in the meantime he had published two other successful collections. He was among the most famous American light versifiers of the first half of the twentieth century. But by the mid-1980s, when I happened across a copy of *Poems in Praise of Practically Nothing* in a used bookstore, Hoffenstein had been completely forgotten.

I had never heard of Samuel Hoffenstein until I chanced upon that copy. The title alone was worth the two dollars I paid for the book. But once I read these funny, philosophical poems, I knew I had discovered a real treasure.

Hoffenstein's verse is witty, irreverent and poignant. The titles of individual poems ('Songs about Life and Brighter Things Yet; A Survey of the Entire Earthly Panorama, Animal, Vegetable, and Mineral, with Appropriate Comment by the Author, of a Philosophic, Whimsical, Humorous, or Poetic Nature – a Truly Remarkable Undertaking' and 'Songs of Fairly Utter Despair') are often rewarding little poems in themselves. Hoffenstein treats life's triumphs and tragedies with a teasing humour and a powerful sense of the transience of things. He's Omar Khayyam with an American accent:

Babies haven't any hair;
Old men's heads are just as bare; –
Between the cradle and the grave
Lies a haircut and a shave.

Hoffenstein was born in Lithuania and came to the United States when he was four years old. He grew up in Pennsylvania and studied philosophy at university. In 1912, after a brief stint as the principal of a public school, he went to New York City, where he worked for a variety of newspapers as a reporter, drama critic and columnist. After almost twenty years in journalism, Hoffenstein moved to Hollywood in 1931 to work as a screenwriter. There he wrote a clutch of moderately successful screenplays, including the adaptation of Theodore Dreiser's *An American Tragedy* (1931), *Dr Jekyll and Mr Hyde* (1941), starring Spencer Tracy, and the film *Laura* (1944), for which he received one of his two Oscar nominations.

Hoffenstein's reporter's instincts make his poems both nicely observed and politically astute. Though much of his verse focuses on domestic affairs – failed romances and unhappy marriages – he did take on larger themes, especially in his last book, *Pencil in the Air*, published just three days after his sudden death from a heart attack:

Wherever the worm turns, he is still a worm.
Power never serves too brief a term.
Where there are willing masters there are willing slaves.
Where there are mass men there are mass graves.

Many of the poems in *Pencil in the Air* were written in the midst of the Second World War. The awful carnage of that conflict only confirmed Hoffenstein's worst opinions of his fellow man. His verse had always been relentlessly morose and fatalistic – romances *always* failed; marriages were *always* unhappy – but the war inspired him to project this gloom on to a global scale.

There was, of course, plenty to be gloomy about. The advent of the atomic bomb made it seem that the human race was entirely capable of snuffing itself out. But on this point, Hoffenstein was perversely optimistic. He believed all our most creative and destructive instincts would ensure that we survived, and he matched with darker humour the darkness of his times:

Fear not the atom in fission;
The cradle will outwit the hearse;
Man on this earth has a mission –
To survive and go on getting worse.

## Dorothy Parker (1893–1967)
### The Wittiest Woman in New York

From 1919 to 1932, some of America's most famous men and women of letters met regularly for lunch at the Algonquin Hotel in New York City. This coterie of wags and wits consisted of playwrights George S. Kaufman and Robert Sherwood, columnists Franklin Pierce Adams and Heywood Broun, and authors Robert Benchley, Ring Lardner and Edna Ferber, among others. Occasionally, people such as Harold Ross of the *New Yorker*, Hollywood producer Herman Mankiewicz and Harpo Marx would drop by. The critic and gourmand Alexander Woollcott was the group's founder and presiding genius. The gang's long, drunken lunches became such a fixture – and their reputation for loud, outrageous conversation such a distraction – that the hotel's owner installed a large round table in the Rose Room specifically for their use. Soon, this loose collection of colleagues, friends and rivals became known as the Algonquin Round Table.

Few of the Round Table's charter members are still known today. But in their heyday in the early 1920s, they were among New York's biggest celebrities, filling the gossip columns with their barbed bons mots and wicked one-liners. Dorothy Parker, who worked as a journalist for *Vanity Fair* and *Vogue*, was the wittiest of the bunch, notorious for the acidity of her wisecracks and ripostes. Challenged to come up with an original use of the word 'horticulture' in a sentence, she shot back: 'You can lead a horticulture but you can't make her think.'

Parker was part of the reason the Algonquin Round Table was also known as the Vicious Circle; the talk could be as cruel as it was creative. But Parker was more than just a smart alec with a gift for coining quips. She was an accomplished light versifier, and her poems read like sardonic agony aunt advice for the lovelorn:

Men seldom make passes
At girls who wear glasses.

Parker had a much narrower range as a poet than Samuel Hoffenstein, rarely straying from the themes of lost love and fickle friendship. But she did share Hoffenstein's rather grim opinion of human affairs. All relationships were doomed from the start, Parker thought, by our self-defeating instinct to traduce and betray those we profess to love the most:

Oh, beggar or prince, no more, no more!
Be off and away with your strut and show.
The sweeter the apple, the blacker the core –
Scratch a lover, and find a foe!

Parker was a modern American Martial. Born in the middle of the first century in north-eastern Spain, not far from present-day Saragossa, Martial went to Rome when he was twenty-four. There he found a sponsor in fellow Spaniard Seneca, who introduced him to the wealthy patrons who later supported Martial's career as a composer of epigrams.

During Martial's time, the job of court poet was still a viable and lucrative one. Writers composed occasional verse to be read at dinner parties or during festivals, and in exchange they received cash, gifts and access to the highest echelons of society. Epigrams are rhyming aphorisms without the philosophical import; Martial wrote most of his to mock his rivals, ridicule his enemies and wheedle more money from his patrons. This little ditty shows that he would have fitted right in at the Algonquin Round Table:

You ask me what I get
Out of my country place.
The profit, gross or net,
Is never seeing your face.

Parker's verse is just as filled with bile and derision as Martial's, but she lifts her poems into the realm of the aphorism by adding a touch of fatalistic philosophy. The title of her first book, *Enough Rope*, pretty much sums up her attitude: given the lengths to which people will go to find trouble, in life as well as in love, it's only a matter of time before we hang ourselves. Indeed, many of the knights of the Round Table came to bitter ends, victims of drugs or drink. Parker herself tried several times to commit suicide, by slitting her wrists and overdosing on barbiturates, but she survived each attempt.

Death was something of an obsession for Parker, as it was for many other aphorists. She used to amuse herself and her lunch companions by devising funny epitaphs for her tombstone, such as 'Excuse my dust'. Her poems are bitter laments for lost loves, lost youth, lost friends. But amid all the wailing and gnashing of teeth, she's the one who has the last laugh:

Every love's the love before
In a duller dress.
That's the measure of my lore –
Here's my bitterness:
Would I knew a little more,
Or very much less!

## Dr Seuss (1904–91)
## A Walk on the Wild Side

Theodor S. Geisel, better known as Dr Seuss, enjoyed a successful career in advertising before becoming a children's author. In the 1930s, his campaign for the manufacturer of a pesticide called Flit was a huge hit. He produced a series of amusing cartoons that featured a suburban couple who fearlessly dispatched swarms of pesky insects with a squirt from their trusty can of Flit. As a result, 'Quick, Henry, the Flit' briefly entered the lexicon of American catchphrases.

When he started writing books, Dr Seuss (Seuss was his mother's maiden name) merged the techniques of the aphorism and advertising – arresting images combined with fresh, unforgettable jingles. Like an effective ad, his loony, faintly

188

lurid drawings and smart though simple rhymes are instantly memorable. And his salesmanship is unparalleled. He was a social critic like the French and Spanish moralists, and whether he's pushing environmentalism (*The Lorax*), racial tolerance (*The Sneetches*) or nuclear disarmament (*The Butter Battle Book*), his aphoristic stories all contain a lesson that's more convincing because of the panache of his presentation.

Yet there's also something deeply unsettling about Dr Seuss. I never noticed it as a kid, but it struck me when I began reading him to my own children: Dr Seuss books are really scary.

His stories often focus on lone children who have embarked on some kind of hazardous journey through hostile and spooky terrain, the kind of eerie place that might result if Salvador Dali designed the set for a Samuel Beckett play. Parents rarely appear except as remote, decidedly unhelpful figures. Kids are on their own in this perilous realm where houses are built on flimsy stilts, ocean waves are sharp as scythes, and even the trees have lean and hungry looks.

Though menace seems to lurk around every corner, Dr Seuss's message is always upbeat. As the wise and wizened old man perched atop a cactus in *Did I Ever Tell You How Lucky You Are?* advises the book's young protagonist, you're sure to get out of whatever mess you're in as long as you keep your wits about you and remember that somewhere someone else has it even worse:

It's a troublesome world. All the people who're in it
Are troubled with troubles almost every minute.

189

You ought to be thankful, a whole heaping lot,
For the places and people you're lucky you're not.

The old man takes the child on a whirlwind tour of all the terrible fates he's been spared. He should be happy, for example, that he's not poor Ali Sard whose grass 'grows as he mows it./The faster he mows it, the faster he grows it'; or harried Mr Potter, whose sad occupation is 'T-crosser, I-dotter'; or forlorn Gucky Gown, 'who lives by himself/ ninety miles out of town' and floats on his back alone in a pool shadowed by the skeleton of some ruined cathedral. The one thing all these unfortunate people have in common is that they're trapped in boring, soul-destroying ruts.

The good doctor's prescription for those leading lacklustre lives is to take a walk on the wild side. In the late 1950s, when he first achieved widespread fame with *The Cat in the Hat*, a lively debate was under way about whether children's books should seek to inspire or sedate their intended audience. Dr Seuss was a troublemaker, an instigator. Throughout his career, he encouraged kids to take risks and make their own decisions, even if it meant annoying their parents. In *Oh, the Places You'll Go!*, he urges a confidence-boosting mantra on the book's main character:

You have brains in your head.
You have feet in your shoes.
You can steer yourself
Any direction you choose.

*Oh, the Places You'll Go!* is another story of an intrepid little traveller who overcomes his fears to make his own way in the world. Setting off alone through a dark, brooding landscape, he crosses vast, desolate cities; rows alone across a treacherous sea; and wanders down barren, empty roads. Finally, he arrives at the most frightening place of all: the Waiting Place, where people wait for 'A string of pearls, or a pair of pants/Or a wig with curls, or Another Chance'. Throughout the whole hair-raising experience, Dr Seuss never misses an opportunity to emphasize that the boy is on his own.

But for Dr Seuss, solitude is a source of strength not anxiety. In the penultimate drawing of the book, the little boy has loaded an entire mountain on to a rickety assortment of axles, struts and wheels and he's pulling it – alone – with all his might:

You're off to Great Places!
Today is your day!
Your mountain is waiting.
So . . . get on your way!

*Oh, the Places You'll Go!* and *Did I Ever Tell You How Lucky You Are?* follow the same plot line as Dr Seuss's first book, *And to Think that I Saw It on Mulberry Street*, published in 1937. In the earlier book, a child starts off on a solitary journey, too – down his own street on his way to school. As he walks to class, he encounters nothing more exotic than an old horse and wagon. Bored by such a pedestrian sight, he imagines that the wagon is a chariot, then a sleigh, then a travelling brass band that's variously pulled by a zebra, a reindeer and an elephant. By the time he gets home at the end of the day, his mental menagerie has had a full police escort and a fly-past from a jet that dumps confetti on a cheering crowd. Yet when his dad asks what he saw on the way back from school, he meekly mentions just the old horse and wagon.

Dr Seuss calls on kids to respond with civil disobedience against anything that threatens to suppress their imaginations. He praises spontaneity and daring, and encourages a healthy disrespect for authority. For him, the way to escape the Waiting Place is always the same, regardless of your age – keep your eyes and your mind open to the marvellous in the mundane:

From there to here,
From here to there,
Funny things are everywhere.

# 7 In the beginning was the Word – at the end just the Cliché:

## The Aphorism Today

Writing long before the advent of the mobile phone and the Internet, Dr Johnson once mused that 'mankind may come, in time, to write all aphoristically except in narrative; grow weary of preparation and connection and illustration and all those arts by which a big book is made'.

Johnson got it half right. Big books still get made, but people do seem to be growing increasingly weary of preparation, connection and illustration. Just look at the most popular forms of written communication today: e-mails, short text messages and blogs. These are all impromptu forms – no preparation is required – and whatever connection and illustration is called for is usually supplied by a quick Google search.

The aphorism might seem perfectly suited to the digital age; the oldest form of literature finds its ideal vehicle in the most modern forms of communication. But mankind is still not writing all aphoristically as Dr Johnson imagined. E-mails, short text messages and blogs share some similarities with aphorisms – they're delivered in short bursts, they're opinionated and often heavy on spin – but brevity is the only one of the aphorism's five laws with which they really comply. There's rarely anything philosophical about e-mails and short text messages, for example, and while blogs are frequently definitive (the political ones, anyway) they get their message across in a shrill, dogmatic and partisan way that is extremely un-aphoristic.

So where have all the aphorisms gone today?

It's no coincidence that Dr Seuss was such a success in the advertising industry, since ad slogans – along with television soundbites – have many of the attributes of the aphorism. Slogans and soundbites obey most of the aphorism's laws: they're brief, definitive, often sport clever twists, and do espouse a kind of philosophy, one associated with a specific product or political party, for example. Neither slogans nor soundbites are personal, however. On the contrary, the philosophies they promote urge homogeneity (of buying or voting patterns, at least) not the iconoclasm and individuality of the aphorism.

One place where aphorisms can often be found is in pop music, the contemporary form of light verse. Bob Dylan is probably the most aphoristic pop star, and 'Subterranean Homesick Blues' contains what's probably his most well-known aphorism:

You don't need a weatherman
To know which way the wind blows.

So even though Dr Johnson's prediction was wrong, aphorisms are still as vibrant and alive today as they were back in Lao Tzu's, Montaigne's or Nietzsche's age. The aphorists of the twentieth and twenty-first centuries are the same kinds of mystics and misfits, philosophers and social critics who've been practising the form for millennia. And contemporary aphorists are beginning to incorporate modern ideologies and technologies into their work – by co-opting the language of ad sales and electioneering, and by publishing their sayings not just in books but on the Web and on giant electronic billboards in Times Square. The aphorism still has a lot left to say.

## Karl Kraus (1874–1936)
### The Bonfire of Inanities

One of Karl Kraus's favourite authors was Georg Christoph Lichtenberg, and among his favorite Lichtenberg aphorisms must have been the one about the impossibility of carrying the torch of truth through a crowd without singeing someone's beard. That would explain why Kraus called the periodical he started in 1899, and edited until his death in 1936, *Die Fackel* (The Torch). It would also explain the incendiary nature of Kraus's own aphorisms, most of which are invectives against the journalism, literature, politics and social mores of early-twentieth century Europe. His attack on the media of his time, for example, is probably just as relevant today as it was when he first wrote it:

195

The mission of the press is to spread culture while destroying the attention span.

Kraus intended to do much more than just singe a few beards with *Die Fackel*, though; he meant to set the comfortable, conventional world of bourgeois Europe on fire. He had a downright Nietzschean disdain for middle-class manners and morality, and took a pyromaniac's delight in setting blazes under society's most sacred taboos.

Kraus was a misogynist who, when it came to sex at least, decried the Church for strapping women into 'the corset of convention'. He heaped his blistering scorn on everything from religion and patriotism to marriage, family life and popular culture. His aphorisms have a whiff of the apocalypse about them. For Kraus, civilization was in terminal decline, mostly because the crassest kind of consumerism was destroying the only thing he thought worth living for: art. Creative people no longer made art, he believed; they manufactured products designed to suit the increasingly bad taste of the marketplace:

There are no more producers, only sales reps.

Kraus once wrote that his business was 'to pin down the Age between quotation marks', but instead he drove an aphoristic dagger through its heart. His goal: to shred the complacency and homogeneity he felt prevented people from being themselves:

How powerful social mores are! Only a spider's web lies across the volcano, yet it refrains from erupting.

Kraus grew up in Vienna, a city that at the turn of the twentieth century was on the cutting edge of the most radical thinking in philosophy, music, art and psychology. Like Lichtenberg and Pope, Kraus suffered from a curvature of the spine that made him a hunchback. His father invented the paper bag and went on to become a wealthy manufacturer, but Kraus didn't have a head for business. Instead, he studied law for a time before turning to his real love, literature, especially the theatre. He toyed with the idea of becoming an actor, but before getting his degree he left university to work as a journalist, a profession he eventually came to despise.

*Die Fackel* became a hugely influential publication, a must-read for Viennese artists and intellectuals. And Kraus himself became something of a celebrity, everybody's favorite cultural curmudgeon. He sharpened his wit against the literati who loitered in Vienna's coffee houses, Austria's equivalent of the seventeenth-century Parisian salons and a precursor to the Algonquin Round Table. But Kraus steadfastly refused to became part of any clique, and to underline his independence often declined to acknowledge greetings on the street.

After the First World War, Kraus began a series of performances he called 'lecture evenings'. Sitting behind a small table, accompanied only by a piano, he gave dramatic readings of scenes from Goethe, Shakespeare and Aristophanes, recited poems by German and French poets, and presented excerpts from upcoming issues of *Die Fackel*. Kraus's recitals became an underground hit, attracting a cult following among the avant-garde. A contemporary of Kraus, who was in the audience for a performance, described one of the evenings like this:

All lights were extinguished. Only above on the table with the green cover were two solitary candles burning. Their flames glittered strangely. Then Kraus came in. Young, with long awkward limbs, nervous as a bat, he moved towards the table, entrenched himself behind it, crossed his legs, smoothed his forehead, blew his nose, collected himself together like a beast of prey about to pounce, listened, waited, opened his mouth as if to bite, closed it again, waited . . . His inner ardour had the same impact as the movement of a locomotive across the dry summer prairie: everything caught fire as he spoke.

Kraus's aphorisms first appeared in the March 1906 issue of *Die Fackel*. He had a variety of names for his sayings: 'Throwaway Lines', 'From the Wastebasket', 'Prejudices', 'Illusions' and 'Splinters'. The last one is the most accurate. Kraus was not shy about parading his prejudices – indeed, many of his remarks about women are extremely offensive – but he had few illusions about the world, and none of his opinions, however inflammatory, can easily be dispensed with. His aphorisms are like splinters because they lodge in the mind's eye, causing tremendous discomfort until you get them out:

Lots of knowledge fits into a hollow head.

Kraus believed that making and appreciating art were the only really worthwhile activities in life, the only way to really see ourselves and the world clearly:

Art serves to rinse out our eyes.

Kraus's aphorisms burn and sting, but in doing so sear away the dried-up old points of view that can cloud vision.

## Antonio Porchia (1886–1968)
## The Taoist in Pinstriped Pyjamas

His friends described him as a saint. Visitors to his modest home on the outskirts of Buenos Aires often found him kneeling in the tiny garden, lost in contemplation of a rose. He had a strangely soothing effect on man and beast. When two thieves broke into his house, he calmly served them tea, after which they left amicably and without stealing anything. Once, during a potentially violent labour dispute, he tamed a vicious dog that a rival union brought along to intimidate its negotiating partners.

He lived a solitary, frugal life, surviving on wine, bread, cheese and the few vegetables he grew in his garden. His dress was eccentric but tidy. In the summer, he wore a pinstriped pyjama top and trousers; in the winter, a simple coat and scarf fastened by a safety pin. He had a peasant's face, rough and deeply lined, but his bald pate and bright brown eyes gave him a Socratic presence. He read little and wrote even less, but

Antonio Porchia produced some of the most moving, luminous aphorisms on the spiritual life since Lao Tzu:

He who has seen everything empty itself is close to knowing what everything is filled with.

Porchia was born in or around the village of Conflenti in southern Italy. His father died when he was twelve and his mother decided to move the family – Antonio and six siblings – to Argentina. The Porchias settled in one of the many Buenos Aires barrios that were filling up with Italian immigrants looking to escape the poverty of their homeland. Porchia took a variety of odd jobs after his arrival, including as a dockworker, carpenter and basket weaver. He eventually bought a printing press and until 1936, when he retired to his garden and to his writing, ran a small printing business with his brothers.

As a young man, Porchia was a kind of amateur anarchist and sometime socialist, taking part in demonstrations for workers' rights. But he was far too otherworldly to get seriously involved in politics. With a group of artist friends, he helped start Impulse, an association of arts and letters, and was for a time associated with the leftish magazine *La Fragua* (The Forge), where some of his aphorisms – which he called *Voices* – were first published.

That, in essence, is the life story of Antonio Porchia. His biography, like that of Emily Dickinson, is almost completely devoid of any signature events. He had a handful of close, loyal friends, but for the rest kept entirely to himself, tending his garden and nurturing his enigmatic musings. He distilled things down to the basic facts of the life that he saw in his garden every day – birth, growth, death – and because all superfluity was pruned away, found the greatest joys in the smallest places:

The little things are what is eternal, and the rest, all the rest, is brevity, extreme brevity.

His aphorisms express an almost Buddhist acceptance of non-attachment as the enlightened response to life's transience:

The loss of a thing affects us until we have lost it altogether.

Porchia was well into his sixties before anyone outside his immediate circle of friends knew anything about his aphorisms. In the early 1940s, he published a collection of *Voices* at his own expense, but the book received scant attention. Then, in 1947, the French literary critic and editor Roger Caillois happened across *Voices* during a trip to Buenos Aires. Fascinated by the book, Caillois was determined to meet Porchia, who he believed must have been influenced by the Taoist sages and more modern masters such as Franz Kafka, who also wrote aphorisms. But instead of the Buddhist scholar he expected, Caillois was astonished to meet a man 'simple and shy, and altogether such that I assured myself . . . that he had never in his life heard of Lao Tzu or Kafka'. Two years later, Caillois' translation of *Voices* into French brought Porchia international recognition and praise from the likes of French surrealist André Breton and American novelist Henry Miller.

Porchia's aphorisms are as direct and unadorned as he himself was, and because of that they achieve an extraordinary depth of feeling and insight. He gets right down to the dark, twisted roots of our deepest emotions and motivations:

The fear of separation is all that unites.

At the age of eighty-two, Porchia fell and struck his head while out for a walk, an accident from which he never recovered. His entire literary output consists of about six hundred beautiful, beguiling aphorisms. Though he spent his life cultivating a very small patch of experience, Porchia made his plot bear extraordinary fruit. It was a labour of love, carried out for the most part in obscurity and with little commercial or critical reward. But as Porchia himself observed:

What we pay for with our lives never costs too much.

## Malcolm de Chazal (1902–81)
### A Dustbin Filled with Diamonds

He hated small talk and loved chocolate mousse. He shunned mirrors – his hosts were required to veil them in his presence on the rare occasions when he accepted a dinner invitation – and shaved each morning in a tiny shard of glass that reflected only a small part of his face. He believed that if you listened closely enough, you could hear the squeaking noise plants make when they grow; he imagined a piano that could play olfactory compositions; he was convinced that technology would one day make solid objects invisible. He spent each day from ten in the morning until two in the afternoon writing and painting, producing up to thirty pictures a session. In the evenings, he would go for a vigorous walk, always wearing the same big black hat, grey jacket and grey flannel trousers. One of his closest friends described him as 'a dustbin filled with diamonds'.

Of all the strange characters who populate the history of the aphorism, Malcolm de Chazal was perhaps the strangest. He was eccentric, irascible and anti-social, filled with an abrasive energy that even his friends found difficult to tolerate. His manner was surly and dictatorial, and he had little patience for anything but the most elevated conversation. But his aphorisms – compressed to an adamantine perfection under the intense, obsessive pressure of his intellect – sparkle with the brilliance of true originality. He once wrote that 'The ideal book has the clarity of a picture book'. And that's exactly what his aphorisms are: elegant word paintings that make previously hidden correspondences between things startlingly visible:

Light shining on water droplets spaced out along a bamboo stalk turns the whole structure into a flute.

De Chazal was born and spent most of his life on the island of Mauritius in the Indian Ocean. The de Chazal clan, part of the landowning aristocracy of the Auvergne and Loiret regions of France, emigrated to Mauritius in the middle of the eighteenth century. The family prospered and became extremely influential owing to its extensive business interests in the island's sugar industry. As a young man, de Chazal was sent to Baton Rouge University in Louisiana to study chemistry in preparation for entry into the sugar trade. But when he returned to Mauritius in 1932, he published a blistering social and economic critique of the indentured servitude at the heart of the Mauritian sugar industry and renounced his place in the family business.

François de Chazal, one of de Chazal's illustrious eighteenth-century ancestors, is said to have dabbled in alchemy and been a prominent member of the mystical Rosicrucian sect. An affinity for mysticism ran in the family. In the 1860s, the de Chazals left the Catholic Church to embrace the religious doctrines of Emanuel Swedenborg, and Malcolm's mother, Emma, instilled in her children her own deeply felt sense of spirituality. De Chazal carried on the tradition. With his metaphysical meditations on everyday objects and his occult theories about the divinity of nature, he was an odd fusion of Gerard Manley Hopkins and William Blake.

Like Hopkins, a Jesuit priest and poet who originally wanted to become a painter, de Chazal was essentially a religious writer. Both men were hypersensitive to the sensual world, the world of colours, odours, shapes and textures. They both wrote with the observational precision of a naturalist and the descriptive deftness of a poet. Hopkins felt natural phenomena, such as trees, waves, clouds and hills, to be expressions of – and evidence for – God's existence. His poems are among the most rapturous descriptions of these things that have ever been written. De Chazal, too, felt a deep correlation between the external world and his inner life. His aphorisms, as well as his paintings, are vivid, brilliantly observed depictions of ordinary things – animals, flowers, teapots, sailing boats, an old pair of shoes. But de Chazal's language is so precise and his imagery so striking that these commonplaces suddenly take a new, entirely numinous existence:

At the height of its trajectory a water jet puts hair rollers into the light's tresses; as the water falls back it undoes them, letting the curls tumble down.

De Chazal and Blake also had much in common, in addition to their shared interest in Emanuel Swedenborg. Both were visionary painters, though each chose to depict very different subject matter. De Chazal found his inspiration in the quotidian, the objects he saw and experienced every day on his evening constitutionals around Port Louis, the Mauritian capital. Blake was a myth-maker, and his paintings were designed to illustrate the scriptures of his private theology. But de Chazal was a theorist of the spirit, too, and his ideas about the correspondences between God, man and nature are crucial to an understanding of his aphorisms.

De Chazal espoused some ideas that can only be described as wacky. In a series of books published in the late 1940s and early 1950s, he laid out a philosophical system he called Unism. The basic premise was that all things are one, everything between heaven and earth is part of a single vast, unbroken continuum. Along this spectrum of life de Chazal identified concepts such as intra-light, the three levels of the brain, the infra-body and the physiognomy of diagonals, ideas that veer off into the esoteric. Some aphorisms read like entries in a Unist catechism, though at times the link between the meta-physical and physical worlds feels strained:

Death is the bowel movement of the soul evacuating the body by intense pressure on the spiritual anus.

Fortunately, you don't have to be a convert to Unism to appreciate the beauty of de Chazal's central insight and inspiration: 'My philosophical position . . . derives from the principle that man and nature are entirely continuous and that all parts of the human body and all expressions of the human face, including their feelings, can actually be discerned in plants, flowers, and fruits, and to an even greater extent in our other selves, animals . . . "Man was made in the image of God," but beyond that I declare that "Nature was made in the image of man."'

De Chazal saw the measure of man in all things, and as a result his aphorisms are almost animistic in the way they impute human traits and characteristics to animals and inanimate objects. For him, the world was anthropomorphic, and with his taut, finely wrought descriptions he sought to delineate its frame. He accomplishes this through analogies that inform even as they astonish, as here where we learn why brake lights are red and flags of surrender are white:

White has the longest arms and the shortest legs: it makes the best semaphore system. Red has the shortest arms and the longest legs: it makes the fleetest messenger.

De Chazal published six volumes of aphorisms and *pensées* between 1940 and 1945, but it was the publication of *Sens-Plastique* in Paris in 1948 which first brought him recognition outside Mauritius. He was fêted by Breton and fellow French surrealist Georges Braque as one of the movement's own, yet there is nothing even remotely surreal about de Chazal's aphorisms. If anything, they are hyper-realistic – intimate, intense depictions of actual physical sensations and objects. Unsurprisingly for a man who lived so completely in the realm of the senses, de Chazal wrote often about one of our most intimate, intense sensations: orgasm. Typically, he regarded sex as both a sensual and an intellectual event:

The act of love turns the spinal column into a finger as if to feel and caress the brain from within.

*Sens-Plastique* has no satisfactory translation into English. An accurate but inelegant rendering is 'sense plasticity'. Perhaps the word 'plasticity' – the ability of a material to continuously change its shape without disintegrating – best captures what de Chazal's philosophy is all about. Since de Chazal believed that nature was created in the image of man, it was only natural for him to sketch out the family resemblances in his aphorisms. For him, flowers had faces and colours had

207

limbs, the world was infinitely malleable, and animal, vegetable and mineral were equally human and equally divine. All created things were linked even as they were changing shape, and this was what held the world together:

Objects are the clasps on the pockets of space.

## Stanislaw Jerzy Lec (1909–66)
### The Eternal Dissident

Ten commandments were not enough for Polish aphorist Stanislaw Jerzy Lec. He was fond of telling friends that he had come up with an eleventh – brevity – which superseded all the rest. Indeed, so great was Lec's insistence on concision that some of his aphorisms aren't even complete sentences:

Politics: a Trojan horse race.

'Life is too short to write long things'; that was Lec's explanation for choosing the aphorism as his métier. And Lec may have had good reason to be in a hurry.

Born in Lvov, a city that in 1909 was in south-eastern Poland but is now part of Ukraine, Lec came from a wealthy and aristocratic lineage. With the dismantling of the Austro-Hungarian Empire after the First World War, his family lost much of its wealth and all of its privileges, a loss that left Lec with a lifelong feeling of imperial nostalgia.

When the Second World War broke out, Lec was sent to a concentration camp in Tarnopol. He survived there for two years, until he managed to escape by donning a stolen German uniform. Back in Warsaw, Lec joined the communist resistance, first as an editor of underground periodicals and then as part of the guerrilla movement. So by the time he was in his mid-thirties, Lec had seen enough carnage and chaos to feel that life in general, and his in particular, was pretty precarious:

Optimists and pessimists differ only on the date of the end of the world.

After the war, Lec remained affiliated with the communists, serving as the press attaché at the Polish consulate in Vienna from 1946 to 1950. Lec loved Vienna, partly because it was once the seat of his beloved Austro-Hungarian Empire and partly because it was the city where Karl Kraus, his literary idol and role model, used to live.

But he gradually grew disillusioned with communism. It was a strange political philosophy to embrace for a man of aristocratic birth who was an admirer of Kaiser Franz Joseph. So instead of going back to Stalinist Poland when his stint in Vienna ended, Lec spent two years in Israel, and his aphorisms became more cynical and sarcastic about his former ideology:

The mob shouts with one big mouth and eats with a thousand little ones.

Lec returned to Warsaw in 1952, by which time he was thoroughly apolitical. He worked translating German and Austrian literature, including Kraus's aphorisms, into Polish, and published four volumes of his own poetry. His aphorisms started appearing in newspapers and weekly magazines, including *Przeglad Kulturalny*, in which he parodied the feel-good platitudes and propaganda put out by the communist party machine.

Lec had to be careful, though, since criticism in totalitarian Poland was not greatly appreciated by the regime. But the good humour of his aphorisms, and the seemingly innocuous imagery in which he couched his dissidence, provided suffi-cient cover for Lec to bend the party line completely out of shape. His attack on censorship seems harmless enough, until you realize that behind this simple image lies the frightening reality of a country without a free press:

The window on the world can be covered by a newspaper.

Lec called his two book-length collections, published in 1957 and 1959 respectively, *Unkempt Thoughts* and *More Unkempt Thoughts*. He referred to his aphorisms as *fraszki*, trifles, and took a remarkably nonchalant approach to their composition, jotting them down on napkins or scribbling them in the notebook he always kept with him. His mischiev-ous word play and deft deployment of metaphor allowed him to land repeated blows for free speech without the censors ever knowing what hit them, as in this denunciation of col-lectivism:

No snowflake in an avalanche ever feels responsible.

Like Kraus, Lec was a satirist. While Kraus targeted the bourgeois values of Europe, Lec targeted the totalitarian state. Strangely enough, both men concluded that the two systems produced similar results – a horrific homogeneity of thought and behaviour that stifled everything that was truly free and creative in people. Kraus held journalists and 'sales reps' responsible; Lec blamed propagandists and their collaborators.

Lec died long before the revolutions that freed Poland and the rest of central Europe from Soviet domination, opening up those countries to capitalism, democracy and the free press – as well as the bourgeois values that normally spring up where these practices take root. If he had lived long enough to see communism implode, perhaps Lec would have revised his grim assessment of where things were going, perhaps not:

In the beginning was the Word – at the end just the Cliché.

## Barbara Kruger (1945–)
### The Art of Accelerated Seeing

It's a Norman Rockwell painting gone all wrong. A little boy, grimacing with effort, clenches his fist and flexes his biceps, while a little girl pokes the muscle with the tip of her finger, an expression of awe and wonder on her face. Across the image in big, bold letters are the words:

We don't need another hero.

211

This classic work from Barbara Kruger is an excellent example of how the art of the aphoristic social critique is still alive and well today.

Kruger was born in Newark, New Jersey, and started out in the 1960s as a graphic designer working on women's magazines. She studied with photographer Diane Arbus and shares Arbus's fascination with the more secretive sides of American life. Whereas Arbus made disturbing images of curious people, Kruger concentrates on the curious attitudes underlying consumer culture by mixing aphorisms with advertisements.

Kruger's work as a graphic designer allowed her to intimately observe how advertisements work by delivering a one-two punch: an idealized scene overlaid with a brief, compelling message intended to sell the advertised product. She says her experience in the magazine industry, and growing up during the golden age of television in the 1950s, taught her 'to deal with an economy of image and text which beckoned and fixed the spectator. I learned to think about a kind of quickened effectivity, an accelerated seeing and reading which reaches a near apotheosis in television'.

Remove the bits about imagery, and this description fits the aphorism, too. Advertisements and aphorisms are alike in the accelerated kinds of thinking they try to encourage or subvert. A successful ad convinces you that you need a specific kind of product; a successful aphorism brings you up short, makes you question things about which you previously had no doubts. By juxtaposing traditional advertising images with her own apposite aphorisms, Kruger makes the viewer stop and think.

Plastered across a close-up of the face of a ventriloquist's dummy is the slogan:

When I hear the word culture I take out my checkbook.

Kruger's mixed messages remind us that shopping is also a state of mind, and her aphorisms make us question the impulses behind our impulse purchases. Ironically, her work has become so familiar that it's now used as raw material for the ad industry itself. Kruger's characteristic red border, her retro images of stereotypical family scenes from the 1950s, her big, bold typography; they're all used regularly in actual advertisements. It's just further proof that one of her best-known works – a hand holding what appears to be a bright red business card emblazoned with a few simple words – is true:

I shop therefore I am.

## Jenny Holzer (1950–)
### Manipulating the Message

In 1993, the German daily newspaper *Süddeutsche Zeitung* published *Lustmord* by Jenny Holzer in its 'Magazin' section. *Lustmord* is set during the Balkan wars and describes a rape from the perspective of the rapist, the victim and an observer. The story is told in brief instalments, each of which is written in red, black or blue ink on to human skin. A card was attached to the front cover of the 'Magazin' which read, 'I am awake in the place where women die.' The red ink in which this text was printed contained a small amount of blood taken from female volunteers, including some from the former Yugoslavia. The mixture of blood and ink caused an uproar in Germany, with people objecting to everything from the health risks (the blood was sterilized before it was mixed in) to the moral offence of writing in blood in the first place.

The *Lustmord* controversy is typical of the way Holzer's aphorisms get under people's skins. Like Kruger, she uses advertisements as her raw material. But she gets her message off the page and into the environment, where we are increasingly bombarded by ads, news and other types of random information emblazoned on everything from T-shirts to billboards to national monuments. Holzer's aphorisms have appeared on baseball caps:

Protect me from what I want.

On sales receipts:

You are a victim of the rules you live by.

On the giant Spectacolor screens in sports stadiums:

If you had behaved nicely the communists wouldn't exist.

And even on condom wrappers:

Men don't protect you anymore.

Holzer, who was born in Gallipolis, Ohio, in the Holzer Hospital, founded by her grandparents, is what might be called an aphoristic performance artist. She studied abstract painting at the Rhode Island School of Design, but shifted to the art of the aphorism in the late 1970s when she began pasting posters of her sayings all around New York City. Holzer sites her aphorisms in places where people expect to see text – such as the big electronic billboards on Times Square, for instance – but her message is so unexpected that readers get a jolt. Imagine the surprise of pedestrians on Times Square watching the headlines and stock prices scroll past when this aphorism slides by:

Playing it safe can cause a lot of damage in the long run.

Holzer breaks the spell that information overload can cast over us by inserting a confrontational message in places where people least expect it. She's deftly adapted aphorisms to new technology by posting her sayings on the Web, where users can change them to fit their own beliefs; by running them across large LED displays in shopping malls and sports stadiums; and by draping them across buildings, memorials and even mountains using massive xenon projections.

Holzer's aphorisms do what good aphorisms have always done: they intervene between you and your assumptions, making you examine them in a new light. She parries and parodies consumer culture by satirizing both its medium and its message:

Enjoy yourself because you can't change anything anyway.

## Make Your Own Bible

Between 1813 and 1820, a visitor to Thomas Jefferson's study at Monticello, his home in Virginia, might very well have come across the former president with a razor in his hand slashing away at copies of the New Testament. As vice-president to John Adams in 1798/99, Jefferson promised a friend that he would one day put down on paper his views about the teachings of Jesus and the Christian religion. He was a firm believer in the former but vehemently rejected the latter, though he was careful not to publicize his unorthodox views. It wasn't until 1813 that Jefferson found the time to make good on his promise.

In the 1760s and 1770s, Jefferson kept a commonplace book that he filled with memorable quotations from his eclectic reading. He took essentially the same approach to the Gospels. He read the New Testament intensively, in several ancient and modern languages, and cut out and kept what he believed were Jesus' authentic teachings and discarded what he considered inauthentic later additions by the Church.

Jefferson included in his recension all of Jesus' moral aphorisms and parables and excluded all mention of hell, damnation, an institutionalized Church and miracles. At the end of the editing process, he said, 'There will be found remaining the most sublime and benevolent code of morals which has ever been offered to man. I have performed this operation for my own use, by cutting verse by verse out of the printed book, and by arranging the matter which is evidently his, and which is as distinguishable as diamonds in a dunghill.'

The Jefferson Bible is one of the most dramatic manifestations of our instinct for aphorisms, the need we feel to create our own sacred scriptures. If the words of wisdom we'd like to live by aren't already set down in one place – in the Bible, the Koran, the *I Ching* or the *Dhammapada*, for example – then we're compelled to compile them ourselves. As the English author and critic Cyril Connolly observed:

Life is a maze in which we take the wrong turning before we have learnt to walk.

Aphorisms help guide us through the labyrinth.

Our aphoristic instinct is behind the popularity of greeting cards, and explains our sudden interest in bad verse on birthdays, wedding anniversaries and bereavements. It's the reason we carve inscriptions on to monuments and tombstones, cut our names into wet cement and tree trunks, scrawl graffiti on the sides of buildings, plaster bumper stickers on the tailgates of our cars, and wear slogans emblazoned across our T-shirts and baseball caps. It's why I started collecting aphorisms on the back of that George Harrison poster almost thirty years ago. And it's what Ralph Waldo Emerson urged when he wrote in his journal:

Make your own Bible. Select and collect all the words and sentences that in all your reading have been to you like the blast of triumph out of Shakespeare, Seneca, Moses, John and Paul.

This book is my bible, a blast of triumph from the great aphorists.

William Blake saw 'a World in a Grain of Sand'. Aphorisms give us the world in a phrase. They are, in Mark Twain's remarkable definition:

A minimum of sound to a maximum of sense.

Once an aphorism makes sense to you, once it gets inside your head and starts striking sparks, it sticks with you for ever. The seventeenth-century French aphorist Blaise Pascal became so attached to one of his *pensées* – an aphoristic account of a religious vision written in 1654 – that he walked around for the rest of his life with the manuscript sewn into the lining of his coat. I've been obsessing about the respective depths of ruts and graves for close to thirty years now, and I still carry that little slip of paper with my wife's riposte to W. H. Auden in my wallet.

The platitudes of politicians, the soundbites of self-help experts, the bromides inside greeting cards – they're all just Alka-Seltzer for the soul. They have a brief fizz, and may provide temporary relief from existential indigestion, but only aphorisms tell it like it really is. Aphorisms are the real elixir of life.

With typical bluntness, Friedrich Nietzsche once advised, 'The author must keep his mouth shut when his work starts to speak.' Before I shut up, there are two people I'd like to thank for giving this book a voice: Katinka Matson at Brockman Inc. and Rowan Yapp at John Murray.

I am also indebted to Andrzej Bobinski in Warsaw for tracking down and translating material in Polish on Stanislaw Jerzy Lec, and to Uki Goni in Buenos Aires and Enrique Zaldua in Spain for doing the same in Spanish for Antonio Porchia. I am very grateful to Marie-France Rose in Paris, Yvelaine Armstrong in Wales and the late James Armstrong, who were extremely generous in sharing their reminiscences of Malcom de Chazal with me. Thanks are also due to Michael Brunton for his invaluable research assistance.

Much more than thanks goes to Linda, Gilles, Tristan and Hendrikje for their love, constancy and forbearance; for life is short and the art of writing books is very, very long.

**Introduction:**
## Guessing is more fun than knowing

**p.5** 'Most collectors of verses and sayings . . .' Chamfort, *Products of the Perfected Civilization*, p. 110.

**p.9** 'In the one, every age in which science flourishes surpasses . . .' J. S. Mill, *London & Westminster Review*, Oct. 1836–Jan. 1837, p. 348.

**p.10** 'The form in which this kind of wisdom . . .' Ibid., p. 348.

**p.10** 'The guiding oracles . . .' Morley, *Studies in Literature*, p. 347.

**p.12** 'A man of most dreadful appearance . . .' Boswell, *The Life of Samuel Johnson*, pp. 13–14.

**p.13** 'There is a peculiar stimulus . . .' Hazlitt, *Characteristics in the Manner of Rochefoucault's Maxims*, p. v.

**p.14** 'A writer of dictionaries . . .' Boswell, p. 81.

**p.16** 'The thought . . . must be stamped . . .' Smith, *A Treasury of English Aphorisms*, p. 15.

**p.17** 'Aphorisms, representing a knowledge broken . . .' Bacon, *The Major Works*, p. 235.

**p.20** The 'true form of the Universal Philosophy', Schlegel, *Dialogue on Poetry and Literary Aphorisms*, p. 35.

**p.20** 'The greatest quantity of thought in the smallest space', Ibid., p. 42.

## 1. We are what we think

**p.30** 'Honor thy error as a hidden intention.' Eno and Schmidt, *Oblique Strategies*.

**p.35** 'Be lamps unto yourselves', Carus, *Gospel of Buddha*, p. 206.

**p.39** 'It is not life and wealth and power that enslave men . . .' *Sayings of Buddha*, p. 14.

**p.39** 'A soldier once asked . . .' Mascaró, *The Dhammapada*, pp. 21–2.

**p.47** 'Muhammad was napping one afternoon . . .' Al-Suhrawardy, *The Sayings of Muhammad*, p. xxv.

**p.50** All Yogi Berra quotes are from Berra, *The Yogi Book*.

**p.53** 'The same Abba Theophilus . . .' Ward, *The Sayings of the Desert Fathers*, p. 81.

**p.54** 'Not taught but caught', Ibid., p. xxi.

## 2. A man is wealthy in proportion to the things he can do without

**p.59** 'Plato entertained some of his friends . . .' Bacon, *The Essays or Counsels Civil and Moral*, p. 340.

**p.69** 'I tried to note down whatever I heard . . .' Epictetus, *The Discourses of Epictetus*, p. 1.

## 3. Upon the highest throne in the world, we are seated, still, upon our arses

**p.76** 'When I considered the important contribution . . .' Erasmus, *The Adages of Erasmus*, p. xi.

**p.77** Proverbs have been preserved 'partly because of their brevity . . .' Ibid., p. 13.

**p.77** 'An idea launched like a javelin . . .' Ibid., p. 16.

**p.79** 'Finding myself quite empty . . .' Montaigne, *The Complete Essays*, p. 433.

**p.80** 'I study myself more than any other subject . . .' Ibid., p. 1217.

**p.89** 'A wise prince . . .' Machiavelli, *The Prince*, p. 34.

**p.89** 'Princes should delegate . . .' Ibid., p. 61.

**p.89** 'Violence must be inflicted . . .' Ibid., p. 31.

**p.95** 'To love oneself . . .' Wilde, *Oscar Wilde, Nothing . . . Except My Genius*, p. 60.

**p.96** 'Natural selection will never produce . . .' Cited in Pinker, *How the Mind Works*, p. 397.

**p.96** 'The dispersed copies of a gene . . .' Ibid., p. 400.

**p.99** 'Energy is eternal delight,' Blake, *The Complete Poems*, p. 181.

**p.107** 'He shut himself in . . .' Chamfort, *Products of the Perfected Civilization*, p. 95.

**p.107** 'What can you expect?' Ibid., p. 96.

**p.109** 'I love blank paper more than ever . . .' Evans, *The Unselfish Egoist*, p. 100.


## 4. Good and evil are the prejudices of God

**p.114** 'The Lords of [Spinoza's synagogue in Amsterdam], having long known of the evil opinions and acts of Baruch de Spinoza . . .' Nadler, *Spinoza: A Life*, p. 120.

**p.116** 'I shall consider human actions . . .' Spinoza, *On the Improvement of the Understanding,* p. 129.
**p.116** 'Whether, in fact, there might be anything . . .' Ibid., p. 3.
**p.120** 'Merchants have a waste-book . . .' Lichtenberg, *The Waste Books*, p. 62.
**p.122** 'The book is intended to convey "a single thought . . ."' Schopenhauer, *The World as Will and Representation,* vol. I, p. xii.
**p.122** 'The real solution of the enigma of the world . . .' Schopenhauer, *Essays and Aphorisms*, p. 31.
**p.124** 'Life is an unpleasant business . . .' Safranski, *Schopenhauer and the Wild Years of Philosophy*, p. 105.
**p.125** 'In my seventeenth year . . .' Ibid., p. 41.
**p.128** 'Truths are illusions . . .' Nietzsche, 'On Truth and Falsehood in Their Ultramoral Sense', in Nietzsche, *The Complete Works*, p. 180.
**p.129** 'Daredevil of the spirit', Nietzsche, *The Gay Science*, p. 9.
**p.131** 'Not by wrath does one kill . . .' Nietzsche, *Thus Spoke Zarathustra*, p. 41.
**p.133** 'God has arrived . . .' Monk, *Ludwig Wittgenstein*, p. 255.
**p.136** 'Tidying up a room', Ibid., p. 299.
**p.137** Trying to 'repair a torn spider's web with our fingers', Wittgenstein, *Philosophical Investigations*, p. 39.
**p.137** 'In the days when I set off . . .' Cioran, *The Trouble with Being Born*, p. 59.

## 5. The lack of money is the root of all evil

**p.140** 'No man but a blockhead . . .' Johnson, *The Sayings of Dr Johnson*, p. 46.
**p.141** The almanac was meant to be a 'vehicle for conveying instruction . . .' Isaacson, *Benjamin Franklin*, p. 96.

224

**p.143** Franklin's thirteen essential virtues, Franklin, *The Autobiography*, pp. 82–3.

**p.145** 'Always do what you are afraid to do', Richardson, *Emerson*, p. 25.

**p.145** 'What is the hardest task in the world?' Emerson, *The Heart of Emerson's Journals*, p. 139.

**p.150** 'How many a man . . .' Thoreau, *Walden and 'Civil Disobedience'*, p. 77.

**p.152** 'Near the end of March . . .' Cited in Richardson, *Henry Thoreau*, p. 148.

**p.152** 'All the branches and none of the roots', Ibid., pp. 12–13.

**p.155** 'I did not know we had ever quarrelled', Ibid., p. 389.

**p.157** 'The immortal axiom-builder . . .' Twain, *The Quotable Mark Twain*, p. 104.

**p.161** 'My future program . . .' Morris, *Ambrose Bierce*, p. 3.

**p.165** 'Laughorisms', Ibid., p. 144.


## 6. Know then thyself, presume not God to scan; the proper study of mankind is man

**p.175** 'I have very little of Mr Blake's company . . .' Ackroyd, *Blake*, p. 312.

**p.179** 'If I feel physically . . .' Sewall, *The Life of Emily Dickinson*, p. 566.

**p.180** 'Enter a spirit clad in white . . .' Ibid., p. 425.

**p.186** 'You can lead a horticulture . . .' Keats, *You Might as Well Live*, p. 46.

**p.187** 'You ask me what I get . . .' Martial, *Epigrams*, p. 29.

**p.188** 'Excuse my dust', Keats, p. 44.

## 7. In the beginning was the Word – at the end just the Cliché

**p.193** 'Mankind may come, in time . . .' Johnson, p. 48.

**p.196** 'The corset of convention', Kraus, *Dicta and Contradicta*, p. 21.

**p.196** 'To pin down the Age . . .' Iggers, *Karl Kraus*, p. 14.

**p.198** 'All lights were extinguished . . .' Field, *The Last Days of Mankind*, pp. 21–2.

**p.201** 'Simple and shy . . .' Porchia, *Voices*, p. vi.

**p.203** 'The ideal book . . .' De Chazal, *Sens-Plastique*, p. 94.

**p.206** 'My philosophical position . . .' Ibid., p. 157.

**p.208** The eleventh commandment – brevity, Tadeusz Nyczek, 'Galaktyka', *Gazeta Wyborcza*, 165, Warsaw, 17 July 1996, p. 11.

**p.208** 'Life is too short . . .' Jan Koprowski, 'Stanislaw Jerzy Lec', *Gazeta Wyborcza*, 242, Warsaw, 16 October 1997, p. 16.

**p.212** 'To deal with an economy of image . . .' Kruger, *Love for Sale*, p. 14.

**p.216** 'There will be found remaining . . .' Jefferson, *The Jefferson Bible*, p. 17.

**p.217** 'Life is a maze . . .' Palinurus (Cyril Connolly), *The Unquiet Grave*, p. 17.

**p.217** 'Make your own Bible . . .' Emerson, *The Heart of Emerson's Journals*, p. 102.

**p.218** 'A minimum of sound . . .' Twain, *The Quotable Mark Twain*, p. 175.

## Select Bibliography

Ackroyd, Peter, *Blake*, Vintage, London, 1999

Al-Suhrawardy, Abdullah al-Mamun, *The Sayings of Muhammad*, Constable, London, 1910

Anon., *The Cloud of Unknowing and Other Works*, trans. Clifton Wolters, Penguin, London, 1978. By permission of Penguin Books, Ltd.

Bacon, Francis, *The Essays or Counsels Civil and Moral, including also his Apophthegms, Elegant Sentences and Wisdom of the Ancients*, William L. Allison, New York, 1897

—— *The Major Works*, ed. and intro. Brian Vickers, Oxford University Press, Oxford, 2000

Berra, Yogi, *The Yogi Book: I Really Didn't Say Everything I Said*, Workman Publishing, New York, 1998

Bierce, Ambrose, *The Devil's Dictionary*, intro. Roy Morris Jr, Oxford University Press, Oxford, 2002

Blake, William, *The Complete Poems*, Penguin, London, 1981

Boswell, James, *The Life of Samuel Johnson*, ed. Christopher Hibbert, Penguin, London, 1986

Byrom, Thomas, *Dhammapadda: The Sayings of the Buddha*, Shambhala, Boston and London, 1993

Carus, Paul, *Gospel of Buddha*, Omen Communications, Tucson, Arizona, 1974

Chamfort, Sébastien-Roch-Nicolas, *Products of the Perfected Civilization*, Selected Writings of Chamfort, trans. W. S. Merwin, North Point Press, San Francisco, 1984

Chesterton, G. K., *'Platitudes Undone' A Facsimile Edition of Platitudes in the Making: Precepts & Advices for Gentlefolk by Holbrook Jackson with the Original Handwritten Responses of G. K. Chesterton*, Ignatius Press, San Francisco, 1997

Cioran, E. M., *Anathemas and Admirations*, trans. Richard Howard, Arcade Publishing/Little, Brown, New York, 1991. Copyright © 1986, 1987 by Editions Gallimard. English-language translation copyright © 1991 by Arcade Publishing

—— *The Trouble with Being Born*, trans. Richard Howard, Arcade Publishing, New York, 1998. Copyright © 1973 by Editions Gallimard. English-language translation copyright © 1976 by Seaver Books

Cleary, Thomas, *The Wisdom of the Prophet: Sayings of Muhammad, Selections from the Hadith*, Shambhala, Boston, 2001. By arrangement with Shambhala.

Davenport, Guy, *Herakleitos and Diogenes*, Grey Fox Press, San Francisco, 1979

De Chazal, Malcolm, *Sens-Plastique*, ed. and trans. Irving Weiss, Sun, New York, 1979

De Finod, J., *1000 Flashes of French Wit, Wisdom and Wickedness*, Appleton, New York, 1897

Dickinson, Emily, *The Complete Poems of Emily Dickinson*, ed. Thomas H. Johnson, Little, Brown, New York, 1960. By permission of the publishers and the trustees of Amherst College from *The*

*Poems of Emily Dickinson*, Cambridge, Mass.: The Belknap Press of Harvard University

Emerson, Ralph Waldo, *Selected Prose and Poetry*, Holt, Rinehart and Winston, New York, 1969

—— *The Heart of Emerson's Journals*, ed. Bliss Perry, Dover, New York, 1995

Eno, Brian and Peter Schmidt, *Oblique Strategies: Over one hundred worthwhile dilemmas*, 5th edn, 2001

Epictetus, *The Handbook (The Encheiridion)*, trans. Nicholas P. White, Hackett, Indianapolis/Cambridge, 1983

—— *The Discourses of Epictetus*, Dent, London, 1995

Epicurus, *The Essential Epicurus: Letters, Principal Doctrines, Vatican Sayings, and Fragments*, trans. Eugene O'Connor, Prometheus Books, Amherst, NY, 1993

Erasmus, *The Adages of Erasmus*, University of Toronto Press, Toronto, 2001

Evans, Joan, *The Unselfish Egoist: A Life of Joseph Joubert*, Longmans, Green, London, 1947

Field, Frank, *The Last Days of Mankind: Karl Kraus and His Vienna*, Macmillan, London, and St Martin's Press, New York, 1967

Franklin, Benjamin, *The Autobiography of Benjamin Franklin*, Collier Books, New York, 1962

—— *Wit and Wisdom from Poor Richard's Almanack*, Modern Library, New York, 2000

Gracián, Baltasar, *The Art of Worldly Wisdom*, trans. Joseph Jacobs, Shambhala, Boston, 1993. By arrangement with Shambhala.

Hazlitt, William, *Characteristics in the Manner of Rochefoucault's Maxims*, Bodoni Series, Elkin Mathews & Marrot, London, 1927

Hippocrates, quotations from the website <http://classics.mit.edu/Hippocrates/aphorisms.1.i.html>

Hoffenstein, Samuel, *The Complete Poetry of Samuel Hoffenstein*, Modern Library, New York, 1954. By permission of Liveright Publishing Corporation.

Holzer, Jenny, *Jenny Holzer*, text by David Joselit, Joan Simon and Renata Salecl, Phaidon, London, 2001

Iggers, Wilma Abeles, *Karl Kraus: A Viennese Critic of the Twentieth Century*, Martinus Nijhoff, The Hague, 1967

Isaacson, Walter, *Benjamin Franklin: An American Life*, Simon & Schuster, New York, 2003

Jefferson, Thomas, *The Jefferson Bible*, Beacon Press, Boston, 1989

Johnson, Samuel, *The Sayings of Dr Johnson*, John Baker, London, 1968. By permission of the James Reeves Estate.

Joubert, Joseph, *Pensées and Letters of Joseph Joubert*, trans. H. P. Collins, George Routledge & Sons, London, 1928

—— *The Notebooks of Joseph Joubert: A Selection*, ed. and trans. Paul Auster, North Point Press, San Francisco, 1983

Keats, John, *You Might as Well Live: The Life and Times of Dorothy Parker*, Simon & Schuster, New York, 1970

Khayyam, Omar, *Rubaiyat*, ed. Louis Untermeyer, trans. Edward Fitzgerald, Random House, New York, 1947

Kraus, Karl, *Dicta and Contradicta*, trans. Jonathan McVity, University of Illinois Press, Urbana and Chicago, 2001

Kruger, Barbara, *Love for Sale: The Words and Pictures of Barbara Kruger*, text by Kate Linker, Abrams, New York, 1996. By permission of the Mary Boone Gallery, New York.

La Rochefoucauld, *Maxims*, trans. Leonard Tancock, Penguin, London, 1959. By permission of Penguin Books Ltd.

Lec, Stanislaw J., *Unkempt Thoughts*, trans. Jacek Galazka, St Martin's Press, New York, 1962

—— *More Unkempt Thoughts*, trans. Jacek Galazka, Funk & Wagnalls, New York, 1968

Legge, James, *Confucian Analects, the Great Learning & the Doctrine of the Mean,* Dover, New York, 1971

Lichtenberg, Georg Christoph, *The Lichtenberg Reader,* Selected Writings of Georg Christoph Lichtenberg, ed. and trans. Franz Mautner and Henry Hatfield, Beacon Press, Boston, 1959

—— in Carl Brinitzer, *A Reasonable Rebel: Georg Christoph Lichtenberg*, George Allen & Unwin, London, 1960

—— *The Waste Books*, trans. R. J. Hollingdale, New York Review Books, New York, 2000

Machiavelli, Niccolo, *The Prince*, trans. George Bull, Penguin, London, 1999

Marcus Aurelius, *Meditations*, Oxford University Press, Oxford, 1998. By permission of Oxford University Press.

Martial, *Epigrams*, trans. James Michie, Modern Library, New York, 2002

Mascaró, Juan, *The Dhammapada: The Path of Perfection*, Penguin, London, 1987

Meyer, Marvin, *The Gospel of Thomas: The Hidden Sayings of Jesus*, HarperCollins, New York, 1992

Monk, Ray, *Ludwig Wittgenstein: The Duty of Genius*, Vintage, London, 1991

Montaigne, Michel de, *The Complete Essays*, ed. and trans. M. A. Screech, Penguin, London, 1991. By permission of Penguin Books Ltd.

Morley, John, *Studies in Literature*, Macmillan, London, 1891

Morris, Roy Jr, *Ambrose Bierce: Alone in Bad Company,* Oxford University Press, Oxford, 1995

Nadler, Steven, *Spinoza: A Life,* Cambridge University Press, Cambridge, 2001

Nietzsche, Friedrich, *The Complete Works of Friedrich Nietzsche*, ed.

Oscar Levy, trans. Maximilian A. Mugge, Foulis, London and Edinburgh, 1911

—— *Thus Spoke Zarathustra*, trans. Walter Kaufmann, Penguin, New York, 1981. By permission of Viking Penguin, a division of Penguin Group (USA) Inc.

—— *The Gay Science*, ed. Bernard Williams, trans. Josefine Nauckhoff, poems trans. Adrian Del Caro, Cambridge University Press, Cambridge, 2001. By permission of Cambridge University Press.

Palinurus (Cyril Connolly), *The Unquiet Grave,* Hamish Hamilton, London, 1945

Parker, Dorothy, *The Collected Poetry of Dorothy Parker,* Modern Library, New York, 1959. By permission of Viking Penguin, a division of Penguin Group (USA) Inc.

Pinker, Steven, *How the Mind Works*, Allen Lane The Penguin Press, London, 1998

Pope, Alexander, *Complete Poetical Works*, Oxford University Press, Oxford, 1983

Porchia, Antonio, *Voices,* aphorisms selected and trans. W. S. Merwin, Knopf, New York, 1988

Richardson, Robert D. Jr, *Henry Thoreau: A Life of the Mind*, University of California Press, Berkeley, 1986

—— *Emerson: The Mind on Fire*, University of California Press, Berkeley and Los Angeles, 1995

Safranski, Rudiger, *Schopenhauer and the Wild Years of Philosophy*, trans. Ewald Osers, Harvard University Press, Cambridge, 1991

*Sayings of Buddha*, Peter Pauper Press, Mt Vernon, New York, 1957

Schlegel, Friedrich, *Dialogue on Poetry and Literary Aphorisms*, trans. Ernst Behler and Roman Struc, Pennsylvania State University Press, University Park, PA, 1968

—— *Philosophical Fragments*, trans. Peter Firchow, University of Minnesota Press, Minneapolis, 1991

Schopenhauer, Arthur, *Essays from the Parerga and Paralipomena*, trans. T. Bailey Saunders, George Allen and Unwin, London, 1951

—— *The World as Will and Representation*, vols I and II, trans. E. F. J. Payne, Dover, New York, 1969

—— *Essays and Aphorisms*, trans. R. J. Hollingdale, Penguin, London, 1970

Sekida, Katsuki, *Two Zen Classics: Mumonkan & Hekiganroku*, ed. A. V. Grimstone, trans. Katsuki Sekida, Weatherhill, New York, 1977. By arrangement with Weatherhill, an imprint of Shambhala.

Seneca, *Letters from a Stoic*, trans. Robin Campbell, Penguin, London, 1969. By permission of Penguin Books Ltd.

Seuss, Dr, *Did I Ever Tell You How Lucky You Are?* HarperCollins, London, 1990

—— *Oh, the Places You'll Go!*, HarperCollins, London, 1990

Sewall, Richard B., *The Life of Emily Dickinson*, Harvard University Press, Cambridge, MA, 1994

Smith, Logan Pearsall, *A Treasury of English Aphorisms*, Constable, London, 1947

Spinoza, Benedict de, *On the Improvement of the Understanding, The Ethics, Correspondence*, trans. R. H. M. Elwes, Dover, New York, 1955

Thoreau, Henry David, *Walden and 'Civil Disobedience'*, New American Library, New York, 1960

Twain, Mark, *Tales, Sketches, Speeches, & Essays 1891–1910*, 'More Maxims of Mark', Library of America, New York, 1976

—— *The Quotable Mark Twain: His Essential Aphorisms, Witticisms & Concise Opinions*, ed. R. Kent Rasmussen, Contemporary Books, Chicago, 1998

Vauvenargues, Luc de Clapiers, Marquis de, *Maximes*, Arthur L. Humphreys, London, 1903

Waley, Arthur, *The Way and Its Power: A Study of the Tao Te Ching and Its Place in Chinese Thought*, Grove Press, New York, 1958

Ward, Benedicta, *The Sayings of the Desert Fathers: The Alphabetical Collection*, trans. Benedicta Ward, Cistercian Publications, Kalamazoo, MI, 1975

Wilde, Oscar, *Oscar Wilde, Nothing . . . Except My Genius: A Celebration of His Wit and Wisdom*, Penguin, London, 1997

Wilhem, Richard, *The I Ching or Book of Changes*, Princeton University Press, Princeton, NJ, 1985

Wittgenstein, Ludwig, *Tractatus Logico-Philosophicus*, trans. D. F. Pears and B. F. McGuinness, Routledge, London, 1993

—— *Culture and Value*, ed. G. H. von Wright in collaboration with Heikki Nyman, revised edition of the text by Alois Pichler, trans. Peter Winch, Blackwell, Oxford, 2002

—— *Philosophical Investigations*, trans. G. E. M. Anscombe, Blackwell, Oxford, 2003

# Index of Aphorisms

236

246